workers@home
Making the Most of Your Time

Erin Thiele

RestoreMinistries.net

NarrowRoad Publishing House

workers@home
Making the Most of Your Time

By Erin Thiele

Published by:
Editorial NarrowRoad
POB 830
Ozark, MO 65721 U.S.A.

The materials from Restore Ministries were written for the sole purpose of encouraging women. For more information, visit us at:

EncouragingWomen.org
RestsoreMinistries.net

Unless otherwise indicated, most Scripture verses are taken from the *New American Standard Bible* (NASB). Scripture quotations marked KJV are taken from the *King James Version* of the Bible, and Scripture quotations marked NIV are taken from the *New International Version*. Our ministry is not partial to any particular version of the Bible but **loves** them all so that we are able to help every woman in any denomination who needs encouragement.

First Printing 1995, Second Printing 1998, revised, Third Printing 2000, revised, Fourth Printing 2001, revised, Fifth Printing 2002, revised, Sixth Printing 2003, revised, Seventh Printing 2004, revised, Eighth Printing 2005, completely revised, Ninth Printing 2006, completely revised, Tenth Printing 2007, completely revised, Eleventh Printing 2020, revised and intro chapters added

ISBN: 1-931800-56-1
ISBN 13: 978-1-931800-56-3
Library of Congress Control Number: 2019914023

Table of Contents

She looks well to the ways of her household,

And does not eat the bread of idleness.

Her children rise up and bless her;

Her husband also,

and he praises her saying:

"Many daughters have done nobly,

But you excel them all."

Charm is deceitful and beauty is vain,

But a woman who fears the LORD,

she shall be praised.

Give her the product of her hands,

And let her works praise her in the gates.

—Prov. 31:27–31

Dedication

This book is dedicated to the many young women in my life, especially my three daughters, Tyler, Tara, and Macy. It is my prayer that the ideas, methods, and suggestions in this little book will help you as you partake in the most important career in this world—a homemaker! It is a job that I have found to be more rewarding, more challenging, and more fulfilling than being a public speaker or an author. I am not a housekeeper, nor are you. We are homemakers. We are what "makes a house a home."

Whether your house is clean and tidy, well-organized and smooth-sailing, calm and tranquil, happy and joyful, will depend entirely on you. Most young women I talk to haven't a clue as to where to even begin. As I began the third revision of this book, I kept you in mind as you begin to tackle this wonderful and powerful position as a . . .

Worker at Home!

*. . . be sensible, pure, **workers at home**, kind,*
being subject to their own husbands,
that the word of God may not be dishonored.
—Titus 2:5

*She looks well to the **ways of her household**,*
And does not eat the bread of idleness.
—Prov. 31:27

Give her the product of her hands,
*And let **her works** praise her in the gates.*
—Prov. 31:31

—————— Introduction 1 ——————

That Too Perfect Proverbs 31 Woman!

The words of King Lemuel, the oracle
which his **mother** taught him
—Proverbs 31:1

Let me begin by saying that the "Proverbs Woman" is entirely fictitious and this woman does not exist, but of course you knew that. Nevertheless, I felt it was important that we all agree that she's simply not real. The reason we need to agree is also simple. It's because this "woman" was my hero and I wanted to be just like her—so much so, that I patterned my life after her. Then I foolishly used her as a measuring stick to determine how well I was doing as a wife, mother and homemaker. And if I had to guess, you've been struggling with competing with this mythical character too.

So, I don't know about you, but this woman has haunted me long enough. All my life, especially my married life, I desperately struggled and clawed through my days to be just like her so I would be "good enough" and "righteous enough" and "pleasing enough" to God.

What I found out only a few years ago was that this is *not* God's measuring stick for women; instead, Proverbs 31 were guidelines that a mother used to instruct her son when **choosing** a wife—a wife who would be his queen. So it's fine to encourage our sons to look for such a wife, knowing even more now than it was then, that this is a woman who is almost impossible to find, a rare and costly jewel. Thankfully, nothing is impossible with God, and as mothers we can trust He will bring the perfect helpmeet for our sons, as long as we are putting our trust in Him.

In this chapter it is my hope that you will understand the truth regarding the Proverbs Woman not being real. I hope it has already lifted a heavy burden and weight off of you, just as it did me, so that you will no longer *try* to be like her. Since now I am free from this burden, it has allowed me the freedom and ease of simply allowing Him to make me over. Though I still do, and will always desire to be well-pleasing to my God, and also my Lord, who is now my Husband, I no longer will believe the lie that I need to measure up. Instead, by living drenched in His love, for more than a year now, I know that there is nothing, not-one-thing, I need to do to please Him—as long as He has my entire heart, that's all He wants. Isn't that delicious?

Now, because of this newfound understanding, everything that I do springs from that love. There is no effort, and no disappointment on my part because, as I said, I know I don't have to measure up! Freedom at last: Freedom to love others and freedom to enjoy living my abundant life!

Forgive me, I just couldn't go on with this chapter without first stating this foundational point again: Your Beloved is crazy about you, just the way you are. It may sound impossible, unreal, and too good to be true, but just remember this, "*while* we were yet sinners . . ." that's when He died, laid down His life, for you and me. We did nothing, it was "while we were sinners." He didn't lay His life down *once* we repented or even *tried* to be good. That's the point. It was when we were rotten, bad, and had no desire for Him at all that He showed His love for us—stretching His arms wide—those same arms He longs to embrace us with throughout eternity. So stop and take a moment and really ponder that truth for a while. There is no greater truth that exists.

Alas, it now seems a bit hard to just jump into what this chapter is all about when you've just peered so deeply into the depths of your soul, but another truth that's freeing is this: Everything that involves us matters to our Lover—everything—even the mundane. So let's turn our attention to a mundane topic, the state of our homes, and how we can enjoy creating a haven for us, our family and our friends. How to simply be the kind of bride our Husband wants us to be, a Husband who wants us feeling free of worry or burdens and inexplicably happy. A bride who feels fulfilled and accomplished—something that women today find impossible to obtain though *striving* for it daily. That's because most women have accepted the lie that by emulating a man and copying what makes a man feel fulfilled will make us, as women, fulfilled. All the while the truth in Proverbs, and throughout the Bible, God has beautifully explained how He created us, different and unique, not at all like a man. "Have you not read that He who created them from the beginning made them male and female" (Matthew 19:4). So let's focus on what does matter to us as women, where we live and read this passage:

*"She looks **well** to the ways of her **household,** and does not eat the bread of idleness" (Proverbs 31:27).*

This verse, which is also part of that Proverbs 31 Woman, is something that I always thought I had *at least* covered, because . . . I was simply never idle. So I felt like I must have both parts covered, I took care of it well because I was not idle. Not so. These are two separate areas that we can use to seek God's help with by asking Him to transform us in this one area of our lives.

Again, there is nothing we can do in ourselves, remember He says, "I am the vine, you are the branches; he who abides in **Me** and I in him, he bears much fruit, for **apart** from **Me** you can do **nothing**" (John 15:5), but *with* God, He promises nothing is impossible ". . . but *with* **God** all things are **possible**" (Matthew19:26).

So why not, using His strength, wisdom and anointing, ask Him to help us to accomplish the task of *looking well* to running our homes, with the desire of creating a haven for our family, our friends and for us to live as His bride? Again, if we *try* to do it within our own wisdom or strength or even timing, our efforts are nothing but futile and worthless. No amount of organizational books or plan of ours will work. Yes, books or articles or television shows are fine to gain knowledge, but only He can fulfill this (or any) aspect of our lives. Simply discuss this and anything with Him, so that He can make it happen—effort free.

Spring Cleaning

While I was flying home from Asia (I mentioned in my first book *Finding the Abundant Life,* I continue to travel for our church through our television ministry), I found I had so much time to think and talk to the Lord about lots of things. One thing that came to mind on this flight was a deep desire that I had to do "spring cleaning."

Confession, I have never really done spring cleaning before in my life, and for some reason I simply wanted to have my house just deep-cleaned and de-cluttered, including and especially the closets and drawers and cupboards. There is something so freeing about having a home that is free from everything that you don't need and/or don't use. It is like a huge weight has been lifted from you and your life. Maybe it was due to something someone had recently said about Erin's *workers@home* book that I've loved and followed for years. Or possibly it was due to something He had up ahead for me (and my family) and the spring cleaning and/or de-cluttering would be the first step.

Regardless of the real reason, I knew since I had been traveling so extensively over the prior year, my home really needed some deep attention. But there is one very important lesson I have learned this past year too, and that is I can do *nothing* at all in myself. Nothing. Prior to this year I put a lot of "me" in everything I did with just a little "sugar coating" from the Lord. But when you are put in a position of being thrust suddenly into become a single mom of big family, plus adding another teenager, then a special needs older sister who requires lots of your attention, then on top of it all, you're sent off to travel around the world half of the time, well, then you find that you are forced to rely on the Lord one-hundred percent, or you simply will go under. That's what He knew I needed to learn—to fully and completely rely on Him—to actually rest in Him even when there was so much to do that you felt that you would never make it or you were about to drop down dead from exhaustion.

So, while flying, I simply told the Lord that I would **love** to do "spring cleaning," then simply surrendered it to Him, not once, but each and *every* time I thought of it. And think of it I did. When I got back home after being gone for almost a month, my home needed my attention, though everything was amazingly clean, even to any unannounced visitor. I thanked Him profusely for the confirmation that as a mother, I hadn't neglected training my children. Yet, I was still determined to let Him do the impossible and provide the time and His plan for a deep-cleaning, if of course, that was His plan. Knowing again that whatever I could *try* to do, rather than waiting for Him, would be a tiny fraction of what He would—in His timing do—I allowed Him to fulfill the desires of my heart. So I waited to be swept into His plan and His flow.

Then suddenly, I saw it start to happen.

You know ladies, this is the way the Lord works—He wants us to wait, then *suddenly* He moves. It is kind of like children who have growth spurts. This is His way and we need to know and understand how He works, so that we can stop fretting when we don't see *anything* happening: **promises fulfilled happen in spurts *after* we've waited.**

Right now I can't remember what room it started with; oh, I know now, it was my girls' room. I'd blessed them with new comforters, sheets, curtains, etc. after their cousin (my niece) left to go back home after living with us for a year. They were once again sharing a room and deserved to be blessed for showing such love to their cousin. God even gave me a head start because while I was gone: one of my children moved out of another room and actually folded their clothes neatly in their drawers. That's when I felt this surge of excitement and energy to make up my four containers and big labels to begin sorting what was in those drawers! Yes, I too purchased Erin's *workers@home* book and am led periodically to follow it as I said. Right then and there, God had put an anointing on or in me, coupled with the knowledge and wisdom that I had gained from this book and from watching all those organizational shows. We were off.

First, I sought the Lord for *where* those large containers were: buckets, baskets, and bags. Here's the thing, at that moment I could have taken over: me, my ideas—my flesh or me trying to follow the book, but I wanted to remain tapped into His anointing so I would be able to give all the "glory to God." And more importantly, end up with the kind of results that makes you want to dance and shout!

Immediately God led me through the house and in the garage, collecting what I needed. I labeled the large sheets of paper: #1 throw away, #2 give away, #3 put away, and #4 store away. In both the #1 and #2 container, I put a large black trash bag to make it easy to move #1 to the trash and #2 to trunk of my car. (If you haven't read Erin's book *workers@home* bear with me or better yet get one; as what I say will make more sense as we go). These containers I lined up 1–4 and explained to my daughters that this is the method to clean *any* room, *any* drawer, *any* closet, or *any* car—*anything*.

So our goal, I explained, was to remove every *thing* from "wherever" they felt led to work: in a drawer, the closet or under the bed, and then ask the Lord, should it be:

#1 thrown away (is it damaged and not worthy to be given to someone?), or

#2 given away (you no longer use it or need it or have outgrown it?), or

#3 put away (it doesn't belong in your room; it doesn't belong to you), or

#4 store away (it goes back in that dresser, or closet that you just cleared out; just not under the bed).

I told my girls that their goal was to try to put as much as they could in #1, then #2 and so on, so that #4 was left with only what God wanted them to keep—the rest, let go of.

To help my daughters I felt led to stop to have something to eat, when He began to speak through me foundational wisdom that I'll share in the next chapter.

~ Michele
Author of RMI's Abundant Life Series

——— Introduction 2 ———

Lessons in Wisdom

*…Do not forsake your mother's teaching;
Indeed, they are a graceful wreath to your head.
—Proverbs 1:8.*

As I said in the last chapter, the Lord wanted me to sit down and during a meal, take time to share some foundational wisdom with my girls. I began by explaining that so much of what we ALL have stored out of sight, like in our drawers and closets, are things we simply don't use or need. And the things we even consider giving away are often damaged and not worthy to be given to any poor soul!

In addition, I also explained that we also greatly overestimate the value of our *things* and feel we either need to #1) "make a buck" (which means make some money for those of you who outside the U.S. and are not familiar with that term) and sell them to a consignment shop or in a yard sale, or #2) we hold on to it until we can think of **who** could benefit from each *thing*, but really it just creates clutter and is buried in a drawer, cupboard, closet or even in a giveaway bag that sits there—never used by anyone, or #3) we simply hoard our things, forgetting that everything we have is His and if we're not using it, we need to ask Him what to do with it.

The bulk of what most of us own, I am convinced, are things that could bless someone else, but we choose instead to hoard it, withholding what could bless someone. I also asked my daughters to look up and mark these verses in their Bibles, "Do not withhold good from those to whom it is due, when it is in your power to do it. Do not say to your neighbor [or friend], 'Go, and come back, and tomorrow I will give it,' when you have it with you" (Proverbs 3:27-28). "There is one who scatters, and yet increases all the more, and there is one who withholds what is justly due, and yet it results only in want" (Proverbs 11:24).

Hoarding is now considered a sickness, but of course like Erin says about most newly labeled illnesses, it's simply sin—like the sin of selfishness. That is why I have come to look at these *things* hidden in our drawers and closets like the talents Jesus talked about that the one **un**faithful servant ***buried*** that made Him so angry. Let's read it together:

"For it is just like a man about to go on a journey, who called his own slaves and entrusted his possessions to them. To one he gave five talents, to another, two, and to another, one, each according to his own ability; and he went on his journey. Immediately the one who had received the five talents went and traded with them, and gained five more talents. In the same manner the one who had received the two talents gained two more. But he who received the one talent went away, and dug a hole in the ground and hid his master's money.

"Now after a long time the master of those slaves came and settled accounts with them. The one who had received the five talents came up and brought five more talents, saying, 'Master, you entrusted five talents to me. See, I have gained five more talents.' His master said to him, 'Well done, good and faithful slave. You were faithful with a few things, I will put you in charge of many things; enter into the joy of your master.'

"Also the one who had received the two talents came up and said, 'Master, you entrusted two talents to me. See, I have gained two more talents.' His master said to him, 'Well done, good and faithful slave. You were faithful with a few things, I will put you in charge of many things; enter into the joy of your master.'

"And the one also who had received the one talent came up and said, 'Master, I knew you to be a hard man, reaping where you did not sow and gathering where you scattered no seed. And I was afraid, and went away and hid your talent in the ground. See, you have what is yours.'

"But his master answered and said to him, 'You wicked, lazy slave, you knew that I reap where I did not sow and gather where I scattered no seed. Then you ought to have put my money in the bank, and on my arrival I would have received my money back with interest.

Therefore take away the talent from him, and give it to the one who has the ten talents.'

"For to everyone who has, more shall be given, and he will have an abundance; but from the one who does not have, even what he does have shall be taken away. Throw out the worthless slave into the outer darkness; in that place there will be weeping and gnashing of teeth" (Matthew 25:14-30).

We usually think of the talents in this verse to be our abilities or special God-given gifts that we could use as a volunteer or just helping our neighbor, but don't.

We sometimes apply the hidden talent's verse to when we bury and hoard the money that could flow in our lives if we weren't so selfish or fearful and chose instead to bless the church, a ministry or people in need with an offering. But what I am talking about in this chapter are the actual *things* that we save and bury because we think **we** may need them for ourselves (or as I also thought, to *save* them for someone else who may want these *things* that are old and outdated "someday"). **No more.** Beginning that very day, my children and I vowed to let go of everything that could bless others: our time, our love, and also the things in our home we didn't need or use. And this also includes any money that I don't need this instant (all the silver and gold is His anyway, therefore, any money I need is right there, all I need to do is give when He tells me to give and use it His way as He leads me), which is why we also will not sell anything either.

Hey, this is amazing, I just remembered that I got a little note attached to a very sizable donation from a church member who said that she was saving the money she sent to me for when her husband came home so that when things went wrong, she could "save the day." She said she'd instead realized that she was not her husband's savior! Her restored marriage testimony just was mailed to me too, and I typed it and submitted it to RMI!

With the foundational plan laid out and all of us in agreement, I began to work with my youngest daughter as we tackled her drawers, then dove into the shared closet. Together, all three of us, removed each item from the closet and put it into *one* of the four containers. There were often temptations on the girls' part to find something and want to take it to a brother (who had been looking for something) or neighbor friend (who they thought would like it), or even to just put it in another room or just outside the door. But I stopped them and explained that this is a common pitfall of most people and why they fail and never succeed in deep cleaning again. You must use #3 the "put away" container and resist leaving the room. You must resist this and every temptation of distraction in order to *finish the course* of action or you will end up with a greater mess than you began with. Though some people would tell you to be sure that you choose a time or day to carve out enough time to tackle a job like this (I would have said the same thing about a year ago), I will now tell you that when the Spirit moves you it is the right time, even when your head reasons that you should do it later at a more opportune time.

Once again, in agreement, and also resisting temptations to leave the room, very soon, with all of us working together, we filled a #2 give away bag, which I closed and put it just outside the door being careful not to block the room's entrance. Each item of clothing that was on a hanger, we looked at and made a *quick* question asking the Lord, "Do I need this?" and then laid it neatly on the bed if we were supposed to keep it, or took it off the hanger and put it in one of the bags when He prompted us to give it away.

The greatest blessing ended up not being the end result of the clean room or what we were able to bless others with. This task turned out to be such a great learning experience for my girls: not just to be good "keepers of the home," but also spiritually: to learn to hear and respond to the Lord. They experienced how to speak to the Lord, rather than to ask themselves, and then respond to His promptings. They also were excited when they would see how He would draw their attention to a tear or stain on a garment that needed to be thrown away, or He would give them instant wisdom that it no longer was their style; therefore, they would never wear it. Sometimes He prompted them to try it on quickly to see if it still fit.

It also taught them to *let go* of what they really didn't need. This is a tremendous lesson in itself. All of us want to hold on and hoard when we need to let go: we won't let go of people in our lives, our money, our things, or even our obsessions that we know are wrong (because they take away time and devotion to the Lord). Another point I would like to make, if I had done this task myself, without including my children, they would have missed this spiritual lesson, and also, they would have missed making the choice to give or throw away things, but that is not all. Never make the mistake of going through other people's things without them so they do not become bitter or resentful when they later find something isn't there (that you gave away or threw away). This is especially true for your husband whether he lives with you or even if he does not.

If you are not living with someone (husband or a grown child), just gather up all their things and put them in boxes to give to them. You can kindly offer to help this moved-out family member go through their boxes, but make sure that they somehow get their things into their possession.

When my ex-husband was gone the first time, I hung onto *any* possession of his as an idol. Imagine. I just could not let go; hence, I had much pain that continued throughout his absence. Had I had enough of the Lord and His love, I would have been able to let go with my heart. This goes for women whose son or daughter (or even mother or father) is gone, for whatever reason: moved away, ran away, or even died through natural causes or suddenly taken from you. We need to let go so that God can fill that void, the void that we fill with *things*. It is like a tumor that is inside our hearts, it has to be removed for it to heal.

Miracle Dashed

Let me jump in here with a short story. Almost six months ago my sister was about to adopt her first baby. She had waited for this miracle for years, but right on the brink, the birth mother chose to keep her baby. My sister was understandably devastated. After I took a lot of time comforting her, I sought the Lord for His wisdom when one day I was convinced she would harm herself. When she begged me to help her, what came out of my mouth was just as shocking to me as it was to her. I told her that she needed to contact the birth mother and bless her with all the baby items she had purchased and gotten as gifts, that these were for *that* baby, and that God would bless her through it. As far as I know she never took my advice; and unfortunately, she hasn't spoken to me since. But this I do know, she is still hurting horribly and has been filling her life with more things, while the baby things gather dust.

Where to store?

Now back to things you have that you are storing for family who are not living with you: if they won't or can't get their things, simply ask the Lord *where* you are to store them. Don't assume you need to keep them. When you get a thought, or picture in your mind, or hear a word, then simply obey it. Don't worry that you may be wrong, He can fix it later; just walk out what you believe He is saying to you or showing you. This is the first step to hearing from the Lord.

Oh, one more benefit of having the person with you when you sort things to give or throw away, if they don't invest in the process, they will not keep it that way! As a mother, these are "train up a child" lessons that are normally not taught any more. You may have not learned them yourself, but that makes learning together even more fun!

Once we had the closet, dresser and under the bed completely emptied, then I asked my youngest daughter to vacuum the room and closet, while the other daughter followed behind and wiped off the closet shelf and wiped out each dresser drawer. Like my girls, you will be amazed at how you feel when everything is clean!! Then the process began to get even better. We then began hanging the clothes back into their very clean closet, clothes we'd laid on the bed, along with a few items in #4 store away (what goes back in that dresser, or closet that you just cleared out; just not under the bed). We then did the same with what went into their dresser.

And as before, I encouraged them to speak and *ask* **the Lord** to help them know what to do as they picked up each item—asking Him to give them wisdom, reminding them of the verse, "If any of you lacks wisdom, let him ask of the giving God [Who gives] to everyone liberally and ungrudgingly, without reproaching or faultfinding, and it will be given him" (James 1:5 AMP).

Amazingly, within the span of just a few hours, while we spent time together laughing, talking and singing, we finally walked out, turned and stood at the door of their beautiful new room! And the blessings didn't stop then either…

Over the course of one week, just before my children headed up to their dad's wedding, the Lord had us conquer so many rooms in our home!! Wow, it was so amazingly freeing!! One room that I never thought of—the bathroom—God had us do too! Like before, through a series of events (when I couldn't find the ear medicine for my son who had water in his ear), I immediately received an anointing that hit me.

As before, I asked my daughters to join me, beginning by removing *everything* from the bathroom into large buckets (and I mean everything). Oh my, what a wonderful Husband I have and awesome Father to my children. He knew how much this bathroom needed cleaning since there had been three girls sharing that space for almost a year! And He added another facet to organizing this space, and that was: sorting "like-things" together. This was something the Lord led me to do while we were throwing most of our empty containers away.

On our kitchen table He led us to sit together then group "like items" together: hair items (shampoo, brushes, rubber hair ties); oral hygiene items (toothbrushes, mouthwash, floss, whitening products); face items (make-up, cleaners, etc.); body items (razors, lotions); girl things (as my girls refer to their *monthly* time); and first aid (bandages, alcohol, antibiotic ointment). And to keep the youngest daughter busy (she tends to wonder off), I had her standing at the sink, washing the plastic containers that help organize the drawers. If organizing "like-items" is not the way your drawers, closets/wardrobes, and cupboards are sorted, then this is how you organize them. Ask Him to be sure.

Once the sorting was all done and plastic containers washed so everything could be returned to their container, together we scrubbed and polished the bathroom—which is so much easier when it is empty—viola, it actually looked like a new home again! Then I had each of the girls take the personal brand of shampoo they each used and put it into the shower. Next, I asked each of the girls to gather their personal items and choose one of each of the four drawers. Then since there were drawers left over, we gathered all the electrically powered items (hair driers, hot curlers, and straightening irons) for the closest drawer next to the outlet and put the girl things (as my girls refer to their *monthly* time), discreetly in the bottom drawer.

Back in the kitchen, we gathered the rest of the items and put them in their groups on the bathroom selves (according to where they fit; based on their height) and LABELED each shelf. Wow, yes, this was "over the top" organization—all because He did it!! We labeled the inside edge of each drawer, too, so I could easily open to see who was not keeping her drawer clean and organized.

This, dear mothers, is something I'd encourage you to do daily: walk through your house "looking well to the ways of your household" and give each room, drawer and closet a quick look so that your children keep it clean. Then soon, you can do a follow-up task just once a week of just checking on everything, and then, soon, just once a month! Personally, I like walking through with my cup of coffee just before everyone wakes up or is just stirring, so I can also dole out kisses to newly opened eyes!

At first, I thought of the follow-up as just another "chore" that I didn't have time for. However, once I set it up as an office notification on my phone, I found that while following up, I experienced the same THRILL I got when we first got it done!! And as I said, with coffee in hand, and doling out morning kisses to waking children, it became something I looked forward to!

Ah, but what about those things that you do find that are out of place in their drawers or closets?

Well, at first, I just took care of it: folded it, put it where it belonged. In other words, it was I who took care of it. Until the Lord convicted me that this was the lazy way. So instead, I just left it and asked the children to fix their mess, as I watched, and you know what? That's the *only* way to rid someone of a bad habit— not fix it yourself—but to lovingly *ask* the person to do it. If you clean or fix something, it won't create a permanent change because there is no consequence. And something else…

The Lord began teaching me, as I have sought Him recently for training my children (since I am gone so much of the time), that unless I also **add** work to whatever they didn't do, we are the ones with the burden, not where the burden should lie, on them. This is new to my child training, and it is working beautifully since this was wisdom from God.

What the Lord led me to do (when I finally got tired of re-doing and re-cleaning) was to pull those items out of the drawers or closets and then ask whomever to put them back neatly or where it belonged. Also, I know when you have more than one child sharing a room it is sometimes difficult to know *who* is doing the dirty stuff with some items left around, but that's when you can call upon the Lord to direct you. He needs to be at the center of everything if we are to live a life of peace and ease! And should you make a mistake, and ask the wrong person, then you can claim double. Isaiah 40:2, "Speak kindly . . . And call out to her, that her warfare has ended, that her iniquity has been removed, that she has received of the LORD'S hand DOUBLE for all her sins." And teach the principle to the person who was made to do something unjust, citing Isaiah 61:7-8, "Instead of your shame you will have a DOUBLE portion, and instead of humiliation they will shout for joy over their portion. Therefore they will possess a DOUBLE portion in their land, everlasting joy will be theirs. For I, the LORD, **love justice**, I hate robbery . . . And I will faithfully give them their recompense and make an everlasting covenant with them."

Oh, one part I forgot, not only should you take a moment to rejoice in what He has done, but you'll also need to **take care of those containers.** Be sure to immediately tie up and throw away your trash. Put the bags of give-away right into the trunk of your car or somewhere you know will ensure it gets **out** of your home and into the hands of a charitable institution (the one HE brings to mind; and never second guess the Holy Spirit if you want to hear from God). The rule is, "Never leave containers *in* the room or it will be a magnet for more things to gather there or worse, someone will look through and take things out!"

IN and OUT Rule

Use the IN and OUT rule to keep each room you've just de-cluttered now clutter free: "one in, one out; two in, two out" when you buy anything. This simply means: if you buy two shirts, give two shirts away. If you buy a pair of shoes, give one pair of shoes away. This rule will keep you from hoarding or cluttering your home again.

Our homes should be a haven that it easy to keep clean and organized; however, apart from Him we can do nothing as John 15:5 says, "I am the vine, you are the branches; he who abides in Me and I in him, he bears much fruit, for apart from Me you can do nothing."

If these two chapters have sparked a desire to change your life, please don't roll up your sleeves and get to work. Instead, take a moment and simply talk to the Lord about your desires—then leave your desire with Him each and every time it comes to mind. Then suddenly, He will move and give you the desires of your heart along with the anointing—giving you a clean, clutter free, organized home while blessing others with the things you simply don't need, and if you have children, a way to train them to always and forever rely on Him!

If you have a testimony of how the Lord has been dealing with you and your home, then either submit a praise report or possibly a What I Learned form to bless everyone who visits RMI! Don't wait, do it today to give glory to the One who so deserves all our praise!!

~ *Michele*
Author of RMI's Abundant Life Series

Chapter 1

Making the Most of Your

Life

Let Her Works Praise Her!

Many daughters have done nobly,
But you excel them all . . .
Give her the product of her hands,
And let her works praise her in the gates.
—Prov. 31:29–31

Anyone who knows my background would think it hilarious that I am now known for organizing and keeping a home neat and tidy! It just shows that God does have a sense of humor, and that with God, all things are possible!

When I married, I could not cook, nor did I know how to keep a home! No one taught me, nor did I have an example to follow.

My mother, bless her heart, loved her children (all seven of them), but since she grew up in a wealthy home with servants, and as an only child, she never learned how to *do anything*! When she was very young (just 16 and still in Girl Scout camp), she eloped with my father, who also came from a wealthy upbringing!

My mother's mother (my grandmother), never allowed her to be in the kitchen or to spend time around the servants. She never put away her clothes or even dressed herself! Her meals were served to her. My father had his meals in the dining room of a hotel where his family lived in the penthouse.

By the time I came along (I am their sixth child), my mother had years of disorganization and burnt meals. My father hired help often, but they were soon dismissed because my mother felt they were an "intrusion," and they only reminded her of her unhappy childhood.

Our laundry room, when I was growing up, was piled high with laundry that was done "maybe" monthly. Meals were always late and always burnt. My mother would cook a dozen meals that were repeated over and over again. Most of us (her children) tried to get invited to a neighbor's house for dinner, or would eat a bowl of cereal!

However, my mother really loved us—we all knew that! It was because of her love that we all turned out more than all right. Maybe we were a bit traumatized by the home we grew up in, but thankfully, most of us can laugh about it now! My sisters, unfortunately, never learned how to keep a home. All of them cook better than my mother, but their homes—well, that's another story.

My brothers married women who kept nice, clean homes (well, at least two of them did). As for me, it was a "God thing" that my home is clean and well-organized with good home-cooked meals. As with every area of my life, God has brought me from tragedy to triumph. I should have followed in my mother's footprints, but God set me free and He is about to set you free too! Thankfully, today my home is always clean and tidy! We have meals on the table at the same time everyday, and thankfully, I have not burned anything in years!

To break this cycle even further, I continue to train my daughters so that when they marry, they will be well-prepared to keep their own homes. All of them (even my sons) have learned to do laundry, to clean, and to cook. It is my desire to encourage each of you to become true older women who will teach and encourage what is right and to help at least one young woman to learn how to make a house a home. Would you do that? If you have daughters, hopefully they are willing to listen and to learn from you. If not, pray and see whom the Lord would have you sow into.

And for those of you who have never been properly trained, I am your older woman! My start proves that no matter where you are, or where you have come from, God can set you free to actually enjoy making your house a home! This book will give you guidelines, but it will be GOD who will transform you and His Holy Spirit that will guide you as you seek Him continually!

My ministry is encouraging women in every area of their lives. Besides my own testimony, my mission is to share principles that will literally change your life, once you embrace them. Here is the first:

"Looking at them, Jesus said, 'With people it *is* impossible, but **not** *with* **God**; for **all things are possible with God**'" (Mark 10:27).

If your problem is keeping a clean home, it may seem impossible with your busy schedule, but not *with* God—all things are possible *with* God!

If your problem is staying organized, it may seem impossible with your personality, but not *with* God—all things are possible *with* God!

If your problem is keeping up with the laundry, it may seem impossible with all the children you have, but not *with* God—all things are possible *with* God!

If your problem is cooking, it may seem impossible because you never liked being in the kitchen, but not *with* God—all things are possible *with* God!

Enter God

No matter what the problem area of your life is, when God enters into that part of your life, it will change! Most of us never rely on God or ask for His help, but instead, we struggle to do things in our own strength by leaning onto our own understanding of what we think we should do. It isn't until we are at the *end of ourselves* that we cry out to Him. Why wait?

No matter how big or how small your problem is, the Lord *wants* to help **you**. He *longs* to be gracious to us! Awesome! "Therefore the LORD **longs** to be **gracious** to you, and therefore He waits on high to have compassion on you. For the LORD is a God of justice; how blessed are all those who long for Him" (Isa. 30:18).

The Bible says that He is actually looking for hearts that are totally sold out to seeking Him, so He can strongly support us in our efforts! "For the eyes of the Lord move to and fro throughout the whole earth that He may strongly support those whose heart is completely His . . ." (2 Chron. 16:9). He wants to give us all of the desires of our heart, from a clean house, to clean clothes, to a home that is running efficiently. "Delight yourself in the LORD; And He will give you the desires of your heart. Commit your way to the LORD, Trust also in Him, and He will do it" (Ps. 37:4).

God loves to show Himself strong on our behalf, especially the most hopeless cases like mine (and maybe yours), so that He can get ALL the glory! "Behold, I am the LORD, the God of all flesh; is anything too difficult for Me?" (Jer. 32:27).

So how did someone like me learn to be known for organization and keeping a well-run home, *while having* seven children of my own and a ministry that operates from our home? By **seeking Him** *and* **through humility.**

Seeking Him

When I was quite young (maybe twelve years of age), I remembered the frustration of not being able to find clothes to wear. My mother would hand us a huge pile of laundry (about once a month), and then we would just put it in *any* drawer where there was room. As I prayed through my frustration (I had accepted the Lord as my Savior when I was seven, even though I was raised in a Catholic home), the Lord gave me a wonderful idea! I thought, "Hey, wouldn't it be a great idea if there was one drawer for tops, one for pants, one for underwear and socks, etc. . . ?" So I organized my drawers, always thinking that I had thought up a new idea! It was years later when I discovered that this is the way most people live!

When I married my husband, he told me that his mother cleaned the bathrooms regularly. I was astonished! "Really!" I said, "How often?"

He replied, "I think, once a week." Then he explained about vacuuming regularly and other daily, weekly, or monthly "chores" (a word that I had thought only applied to people living on a farm).

The knowledge was helpful, but since I didn't grow up in an environment like that, I didn't know how to incorporate working it into my everyday life. As I prayed, the Lord brought to mind a system that my brother taught me about using 3x5 cards that helped me to get straight "A's" in college. That's how my 3x5 card method began. (You will read about the method in a future chapter.)

Humility

Humility was how I learned to cook. During the two years, when I was seeking God to restore my marriage, I did a LOT of fasting. It says in Scripture that fasting humbles the heart.

It was easy to begin learning to fast during this period of my life, because I really *couldn't* eat! I hurt too much since my husband was living with another woman and I was left with four little children to care for alone. In our ministry, we call this the "infidelity diet."

So, since I "couldn't" eat, I thought I would make good use out of it and fast for a purpose. While fasting, I found myself excited for the first time about cooking and feeding my children. This had to also be a "God thing"—I found pleasure in watching *them* eat!

In addition, for the first time, I admitted that I was not a good cook. I had already begun my ministry to women, and during the meetings, I would often say that I couldn't cook. The result was that so many women came to my aid to help me to learn! They gave me easy recipes and even stood next to me to show me how to do simple things like peel an apple to make an apple pie.

By the time God restored my marriage two years later, God had transformed me into a good cook!! My husband returned home to a wife who could cook (with many other changes). God was even faithful to change my husband, who, because of the many trials he had while living with the OW (other woman), which God tells us will happen to a man in adultery, he learned to fix things in the house and in the car! Isn't God so faithful?!

The lack of humility was not the only thing standing in my way with regard to cooking. The root cause was the belief and acceptance of a lie. I will tell you honestly that I never wanted to be a good cook, because I believed all good cooks were fat! My mother was a large woman, and I didn't want to add "being a good cook" to my genetics that leaned toward obesity.

If that is your concern, then let the truth set you free—that is a lie from the pit of "you know where!" There is NO curse that can touch you because that was broken when the Lord died on the cross for you and me. If you are a child of God, the curse has no effect on you, unless you accept it! Here's proof:

A few years ago, actually right after my 40th birthday, I began to have trouble with my weight. When my seventh child was born, and after our eighth (whom I sadly lost), I was unable to lose the weight that I normally could lose after a birth or a miscarriage. That is when my brother and sister began to insist that I accept the curse that our family has with a metabolism and thyroid disorder. They were right, I did have ALL the symptoms, but I refused to accept it!

One day, I stood in front of the mirror and ***cried out to God*** to make me thin. I repented of all the times that I did not have compassion on women who were overweight, and for not giving God the glory for being able to remain thin with so many children (I went over 200 pounds with all but one pregnancy!). By the grace of God, I was able to be very thin by the time each baby was just a few months old. After I had repented of everything that the Lord brought to mind, I then gave my weight and size to Him!

The hardest part was not trying to *help* God to do it. Thoughts of different kinds of diets, drinking more water, exercise, etc., etc. would run through my mind. For three to four months, I was "tempted" to try to help God when suddenly, things just started to *happen!*

I began to crave different foods, and I started to feel that my jeans were looser. I NEVER got on the scale again, so I wasn't tempted to get excited with my weight loss and celebrate with overeating. Nor did I want to feel depressed if I had gained weight. I left my size to the Lord, for Him to do it and to give me the desires of my heart—which was to be a "*loose* size 10."

Honestly, I cannot tell you how God did it. Things changed from day-to-day, but one thing is for sure—He was in control! There was no worrying, no fretting, no hard work. There was no counting carbohydrates or calories. There was no hunger and no denying myself, which usually resulted in an *obsession* for food.

Only four months later, I was a loose size 10. I started at a very tight size 16, which for my height of almost five foot ten isn't *that* bad, but it wasn't me, nor was it the "desire of my heart"! But did you know that God LOVES to give us above and beyond what we could ever hope, think, or ask for? He does! I continued to shrink, and found myself at a size six! This was the size that I was when I accompanied my husband to his high school reunion! Isn't God so good?!

May I just add a short epilogue to give my Beloved even more praise? It was at my ex-husband's high school reunion that sparked an old flame with his high school sweetheart whom he married within the year of divorcing me. Though I have had conversations via email, I have yet to see her again after she became involved with my husband. The last time she saw me, I was tanned, gorgeous, and a size 6!! Isn't the Lord just too good to be true?

I am telling you this to encourage you to TRUST God to do it! **Cry out to Him,** and then stand back and let Him do it! That is probably the hardest part!! No matter what area of your life you are struggling with, if you cry out to God, surrender the problem to him, and then *resist* trying to help Him (which usually lasts through about four months of temptations and testing)—God will do it *for* you, and with no sweat! Instead, all, and I mean ALL, the praise and glory will go to Him!

As I said earlier, this book and all my books give you guidelines, wisdom, and knowledge—but it will be God who will do all the changing. Then, give HIM the glory!! That's all that He wants for blessing you!!

However, I hope you noticed from the beginning of my weight loss testimony that the first step was repentance. God would not move in this area of my life until I first repented of lacking compassion for women who were over-weight. Secondly, I needed to repent for not giving God the glory for what He had done by keeping me thin after each pregnancy.

When asking God "why" there are so many homes with chaos and untidy tendencies, God has brought one Scripture to mind as the root cause. It is not only a lack of knowledge, or a lack of humility (or believing a lie, as it was in my case), but it is also rooted in a common sin that is rampant in our feminist and "me first" society!

Selfish Ambition

Is there really *anyone* who would not want to have a home that is clean and runs smoothly? However, most homes that I see are not so blessed. As I said in the dedication, whether or not your house is clean and tidy, well-organized and smooth-sailing, calm and tranquil, happy and joyful, will depend entirely on **you**.

Some of you have chosen a life that is much too busy with outside activities. Your home reflects the rat race with chaos and disorder! The root cause for many of us can be found in James 3:16 when it says, "For where *jealousy* and *selfish ambition* exists, there is **disorder and every evil thing**."

When "my own agenda" is first and foremost in my life above God's plan, which gives me the responsibility to keep my home clean and running efficiently, then that is selfish ambition. Anytime this creeps into my life (usually brought on by selfishness or self-pity), then my life and my home are disorderly and evil runs rampant!

Most women who work outside the home do not have a well-run home, instead, it is usually filthy! But surprisingly, even stay-at-home moms can have a home that looks the same way: untidy, unclean, and disorganized.

It could also be the unconfessed sin of jealousy or envy that keeps your home and your life in constant disorder. Again, the verse says, "For where *jealousy* and selfish ambition exist, there is disorder and every evil thing" (James 3:16).

We see someone who has what we think we should have, instead of what God wants to give us. This causes us to be involved in activities that will make our lives, our children's lives, and our family's life just too busy to keep up with!

Are you trying to keep up with your friends or to impress your family, rather than trying to simply rest in the Lord? If you are a man-pleaser, trying to gain the approval or praise of others, **you will be worn out**. Know who you are in Jesus. Know His unconditional love. You don't need to do ONE thing today to gain His love—the Lord and His love is there for you unconditionally!

God is NOT a God of *confusion*. We know God is not a God of confusion; therefore, He does not want us to live in confusion or disorder. First Corinthians 14:33 says, "For God is **NOT a God of** *confusion* but of peace . . ."

The most important thing you can do to be a happy and contented "worker at home" (whether you also work outside your home, or whether you are blessed to stay-at-home) is to find the peace in KNOWING that the Lord is happy, pleased, and in love with you, no matter what you do or don't do today. Find that peace, and rest in His love for you. Once you feel His love and His peace, then everything will begin to fall into place.

You will find that your life will begin to change. Some things will go and will be replaced with other things. Everything will begin to get into the proper order, and with it, PEACE will remain. Your joy will overflow to your family. Your contentment will strengthen every area of your life and each of your relationships.

As I conclude this first chapter, I pray that before you read any more, you will read and re-read this foundational chapter.

———————— Chapter 2 ————————

Making the Most of Your

Space

Removing the Clutter

The way of the sluggard
is as a hedge of thorns,
But the path of the upright is a highway.
—Prov. 15:19

This used to be Chapter 7 a few revisions ago, but it was moved to the front of the book. God began prompting me to move it to the second chapter when I saw so many women, who read the *workers@home* book, who **began** by removing the clutter from their homes. Though it wasn't originally written that way, this obviously is God's way—this is where *He* wants to begin in *your* life as well. Take time to read the chapter all the way through, and maybe even a second or a third time, before you take any action. De-cluttering is a principle that you need to *learn*. It is not merely a task to undertake.

I have been passionate about organization for many, many years. Yet, when I read my first book on de-cluttering my home, it took a few days for it to really sink in. That's when it all began to make sense. I thought to myself, "For all these years, I have really been organizing and reorganizing **clutter!**"

Clutter is an Encumbrance

What exactly is clutter? Clutter is any *stuff* that you hang onto that you *honestly* no longer use. It might be things that you *think* you might use in the future. However, stuff that you are really not using, currently, is nothing more than hoarding, which leads to selfishness. Clutter then, is made up of the things you really need to "let go" of. They are the things that are slowing down your race; they are the encumbrances that make you feel tired and overwhelmed. "Therefore, since we have so great a cloud of witnesses surrounding us, let us also lay aside every **encumbrance** and the sin which so easily *entangles* us, and let us run with endurance the race that is set before us . . ." (Heb. 12:1).

If you have things that you are not currently using (I'm speaking of the things that are nice and have some sort of worth), then by giving them away (to even someone whom you will never know or meet when, for instance, you give it to a thrift store), you are blessing someone who may never have what they *need* because you were not able to "let go"—simply because **you** still *want* it.

Not only will you be blessing someone else, but you will also reap the benefits of having more drawer space and/or closet space! The greatest reward is how incredibly easy it will be for you and your family to keep your de-cluttered home clean!

My family has literally (after de-cluttering) been left with about *half* of what we owned, and we didn't miss one thing! Each time we de-clutter (the last two times because of moving), there was a freedom that set in and settled over our entire family. And if that were not enough, your house stays neat and tidy until you need to de-clutter again.

You may be more than willing to let go, but typically your children are not. Children are selfish by nature. (We will discuss husbands who can't let go later.) Even though your children may have outgrown the clothes or toys, most children still want to keep them!

Another note that leads to clutter, when passing down unused or outgrown items to younger siblings, it is wise to make sure that whatever it is will be worn, played with, or read by the younger sibling. All your children are different, not all the clothes look equally good, and not all toys are as enjoyable to each child.

Also, in regard to passing down clothes, saving something for a year is fine, but any more than that and the style probably will be outdated, which again leads to clutter.

When my babies were coming "fast and furiously" (not in regard to the speed at which I labored, but how close they were apart in years), I was given boxes and boxes of baby clothes from a lady who had lost her husband. I added what she gave me to what I was already storing. I carefully put the boxes and rubber buckets into storage, but to my horror, when I was pregnant and opened the box, they were mildewed and spoiled beyond salvage.

I was ashamed, because although I had heard the message of "letting go" of what I didn't need, I hadn't heeded the principle. All I could think about was how many mothers, maybe even young unwed mothers, could have benefited from what was now destroyed because of my hoarding what I didn't need. But God is good!! After I repented and shared my sins with many other women, when the subject came up, God blessed me with all brand new clothes for my next baby when I "just happened" to walk into a store when everything was more than 75 percent. off!

The Objections

Now you (or your husband) may be thinking, "Well, I know what will happen if I get rid of all our clutter—I'll just run out and buy more stuff to fill up the empty space." But I haven't, the ladies that followed this book haven't, and you won't either when you experience the freedom from clutter. I also purchase about one-third to one-fourth of what I used to buy. When we de-cluttered, it was difficult watching all your stuff getting thrown away or given away. I thought of how much money we had spent for all that stuff, which taught me to purchase wisely rather than impulsively!

Since the first episode of de-cluttering, when my family and I go shopping, we keep in mind whether or not what we buy will really be used or worn. This also goes for gifts that we buy for one other. Rather than just getting "something," we make sure that it is what the other person really needs or wants.

A lot of what we threw away or gave away was given to us as gifts, a lot of it was someone else's stuff that people gave us that we felt too guilty to get rid of, and the rest, or the majority, of it were things that we had purchased that we really didn't **need** but wanted at the time.

No matter *how* you or I get something, it is foolish to keep whatever it is when we really don't use it. Therefore, it is *very* good for you and me to get rid of anything we don't use so that we can bless someone else *and* so we can free up the space in order to keep our homes tidy (and not simply to fill the space again).

Since my first de-cluttering experience, I began avoiding a lot of stores where I used to just "browse" just to buy "something." Because of de-cluttering my house, I had finally begun to buy *wisely*. Now when I pick up most things to look at, I ask myself, "Do I really need this?" and "How soon before this gets into one of the give-away bags?"

Just because something is a "good buy" doesn't mean that you should buy it. I know it is difficult to pass up a bargain, but if you don't really need it, you won't use it. And if you don't use it, it will clutter your home, which is not worth the "sale" price you pay. Instead, wait and pray for things that you really need.

I pray about every need I have. I cannot tell you how often, the very next day, I will just walk into a store, and there is what I have prayed for at an incredible, unbelievable price. Just last Saturday, as I was searching for a sweater for my daughter to wear for church the next day, I noticed she had only one sweater that fit her. So I prayed, and the next day, on Sunday, I "just happened" to walk right into a store where I was able to get four sweaters for the price of one! Always tell the Lord what you need and He will provide it supernaturally!!

And finally, most women feel that they don't even have the time to de-clutter. Truthfully, you don't have the time not to! The time you take to de-clutter will make you feel as if you have lost 50 pounds! Your life feels skinny and free! You'll feel like a new woman! You'll be happier, and your family will be happier too with the change!!

Once you are in the right frame of mind (you may need to pray and read this chapter again), you are ready to begin.

The Tools You'll Use to De-Clutter

To de-clutter your home you will need:

1. Five buckets, boxes, or containers (I often use laundry baskets).
2. Five pieces of notebook paper (Different colored paper is better).
3. A black marker or dark colored crayon.
4. 3x5 cards.
5. Large *black* trash bags (four to begin with).

Five signs. These signs will help you sort what you have into five categories:

1. Throw away.
2. Give away.
3. Put away.
4. Store away.
5. Put back.

Make five signs with your paper and marker using the list above. I bring a trashcan in and label it "Throw away.". Next to it, I use a laundry basket or box and put an opened black trash bag in it to lend the bag support and label it "Give away." Next to this, I put another laundry basket or box and label it "Put away." Next to this, I put a box with a lid and label it "Store away.". And finally, I put the last laundry basket or box and label it "Put back," (but I don't place a black trash bag in it).

Begin by *emptying* out *one* closet, or *one* drawer, or under *one* bed, or off *one* of your shelves. *Start with something that you know you can finish easily.* (If you choose a closet, start with the floor.) Pick up an item and put it into one of the five containers. Your goal is to try to put the *most* in "Throw away," then "Give away," followed by "Put away," "Store away" or "Put back."

Decide what that drawer, closet, or shelf is going to store in that space. In other words: What really belongs in that closet, drawer, or on that shelf that you are de-cluttering? So when you come to an item that belongs in that closet, drawer, or on that shelf, **place it in "Put back."** This should be simple enough!

Just begin by picking up one item and put it into a container. If you or one of your children comes to something that you are just not sure of, stop and pray, asking the Lord for wisdom and discernment. Listen for that *still, small voice,* and then respond to His leading—whatever it is. Trust that if you do put it in the wrong container, the Holy Spirit will prompt you to pull it out and place it where it belongs. I promise that He will when He sees that you are doing your best to follow His leading. However, make sure that when you do go back to retrieve something, it is not because you began to "lean onto your own understanding" or began to reason why you might want to keep it instead of giving it or throwing it away.

Once everything in that closet, drawer, or shelf is empty, wipe it out, or sweep it out, and put back **only** what belongs there: what you have in your "Put back" container!

And, don't make the mistake of purchasing any more plastic storage containers, hangers or other organizational paraphernalia to help to keep that space organized. Only buy it *after* you see what you have left. You will be amazed that once you have de-cluttered, you will find that you no longer need more hangers or more organizational containers!

Your goal is to take *everything* out, vacuum it out, and/or wipe it down. Then put only the items that belong in that space, back in that space.

Follow Through

The final step is to **follow through** by dealing with the other containers.

First, take the "Throw away" items immediately to the trashcan. Next, put the "Give away" items into your car so you can send it to the local thrift store. The "Put away" container can be carried throughout your house, putting each item away into the right room. Put away those things that you, or someone else, placed there by mistake, or more often than not, by convenience.

Remember: you should pitch (throw away) anything and everything that is broken or stained. Too often, we keep things that need to be repaired but are never repaired. Don't put too much value on junk, it will weigh you down, so lay aside each encumbrance so that you can run the race of your life!

Now, for those things that need to be "Stored away," such as seasonal items, a family keepsake or clothing items that will be used once a year. We will now use a 3x5 card for each item that you place into a storage box.

Store It

Store it. The "Store away" items will be put into some sort of a container—but as you do this, write down *every* item on a 3x5 card! It doesn't matter what is in each box; you don't need to try to put "like items" together for this foolproof storage method.

Of course, most of us keep our Christmas things together, but sometimes in January, we usually find an item that has missed our Christmas storage. Go ahead and put it into *any* storage box, because you will mark on the card where that item is located. Next Christmas, your cards will remind you where the missing item(s) can be found. To remind me even further, I put a sticker on a Christmas 3x5 card, to remind myself that there are missing items stored elsewhere. Then you can remove them from one box and put them back in the original box at the end of that Christmas! Simple.

The type of container doesn't matter as long as it has a cover to keep out the dust. You can use any existing cardboard box or plastic container. If you are going to go out and buy a container, clear containers are the best since you can look into them, making it simpler to spot something stored there. But again, with this method you can use any box you have or find, no matter what the size or shape is.

Storage 3x5 card. Number each 3x5 card in the *upper **left*** corner, and number the corresponding box on several sides—i.e., "C-1" would be your first Christmas box, "M-1" for your first maternity clothes box, etc.. For miscellaneous storage, I write "S-1," and for old home school curriculum that I am not using that year, I label it "HS-1."

Next, write down where you will store it in the *upper **right*** corner—i.e., garage-west side, attic over the living room, or under my bed. This will help you, your husband, or son find the box more easily.

If your box is a leftover VCR box or a stroller box, indicate that on the card under where it is located to make it very easy to find. The most important point with this principle of storing items is to ***write down EVERY item you place in the box***.

If possible, before you put more into your storage areas (especially if you are storing it under a bed or in a closet), it would be wise to open up previously stored boxes (stored before this system), and make a 3x5 card for each box. And while making the 3x5 card, don't miss the opportunity of throwing or giving away anything that you no longer need.

Warning: Stay away from the Christmas boxes or baby clothes for the moment! Wait until Christmas and "clean sweep" your stuff. I got my Christmas decorations down to half, right after I got motivated writing this updated portion of the book. Praise God! This year, I will go through our Christmas boxes again. For the past two years, no one felt like putting up anything except the tree and a wreath on the door (we kept our Nativity set up since I wanted to remember our Savior's birth all year long). Therefore, it is time to de-clutter and bless others with our unneeded items.

Finally, if you ever move a box or remove an item, adjust your card. Your cards should be kept up-to-date by pulling out the cards, when you pull out a box. The "storage" cards should be kept in the *back* of your 3x5 card file with a section divider that you mark STORAGE. I have had this method for YEARS. Just like everything, it is something that you learn and practise until the way you do it becomes a habit. Not only will you have order and peace in your home, with more room in your closets and drawers for things you actually use, you will be teaching your daughters how to be a keeper of her home!

More About the De-cluttering Method

This is the method for de-cluttering anything and everything.

Once you make your sorting sheets, save them until your entire house is de-cluttered and easy to keep clean! I started saving mine in the back of my shopping list and meal planner clipboard so that I could use them again and again.

This method brings so much freedom that when I feel as if I need a pick-me-up, I just go to a cupboard, drawer or closet and start to de-clutter! Honestly, it never fails, once that closet, drawer, or shelf is cleaned out, it will give you such a joyful feeling. Once you get hooked, you will find yourself going to another closet, drawer, or shelf whenever you have any time!

Should you "Give it" away to someone special or to a charity?

If the Lord brings someone to mind when sorting, then put it in a bag labeled with their name on it. If not, then just give it to the poor. God really began to pour out His blessings on our family when I stopped trying to make a "buck" by bringing it to consignment shops or having a yard sale. When I simply blessed the poor with the things I didn't have use or space for, God blessed me with things I needed and wanted at INCREDIBLE bargains!

Rules. Never go back into a bag. Give away or throw away all your bags as soon as you are done. Put the "Throw away" items out with the trash immediately. Put the "Give away" bag into your car along with a note on the driver's seat to drive to the nearest drop box or thrift store. Once you, your children, or your husband begins to DIG through what is in there, it will undo all your hard work. This is why I recommend BLACK bags, because the white ones often show a *glimpse* of something of interest, which inevitably will draw a person in for a second look.

On the subject of husbands and de-cluttering: this can be a touchy subject. Thankfully, the situation that I had with my ex-husband was that I was the one who wanted to "let go" of stuff and my ex-husband needed to keep things. So, I became an instant authority on what ***not*** to do! My very first mistake (though there have been many others) is when I attempted to *help* him clean out his wallet, many, many, many years ago. When we were married less than a year, I thought I should rescue him, since it was so thick that it was almost a square cube! What was the result of my helping him? For almost 15 years (until he began to lose a bit of his memory), if he was *ever* missing *anything,* he was sure that it was something **that I had thrown away** from his wallet! Mistake. Do not sort your husband's stuff: not his wallet, "junk" drawer, or desk. You can sort it, but never throw anything out without him seeing it first. And if he says "no," then box it up and store it (just be sure to use the 3x5 card method so you can find anything that belongs to him in an instant).

Professional organizers have a method that they use for things that people have trouble parting with. They put it in a box, and then, if you haven't needed to use it (most people have no idea what's even in the boxes), they pitch the entire box. Even if you pulled it out a year later, when you go through it after a year, it would be much easier to get rid of stuff that you haven't seen or thought of for over a year.

Personally, I don't use that method because when I tried it, and the year was up, he didn't want to waste his time to look at his old stuff; your husband might be the same way. So instead, I waited until we moved, when he knew he was going to have to pick each of those boxes up, load them in a truck, and unload them at our new house. He instantly got very motivated to get rid of stuff that he didn't need, and I didn't have to say a thing! Isn't God just so good?

Does that mean that we didn't have boxes of his stuff at our new house? No, my ex-husband had lots of boxes filled with his stuff that are probably still up in our attic, but I don't let it bother me. I chose to respect his position as the head of our household when he was here. I chose to teach my children not only to respect their father by *my* actions and attitude, which in turn, resulted in them respecting me! If I were to undermine his authority, I would also have been undermining my own.

Now, for things that are not directly your husband's personal items: some men want a handle on all the household issues, while some don't want to be bothered. But one thing is the same, whichever you have been *blessed* with—you wish you had the other! My ex-husband was a man who wanted to be in control of anything and everything. I always "hoped" that some day he would leave it up to me. That day came when he left me for his high school sweetheart. Instead of being hurt, ashamed or any other negative feeling that many women feel, I chose to look for each blessing since the Lord promises us that, "all things work out for our good when we love Him and want to know His purpose in it." To be able to throw out and give away things we don't need, without the fear of having a husband who will get angry is a blessing. And when I do come across boxes of stuff from my ex-husband, I set it aside for him to cart away during his next visit to see the children. Isn't the Lord just too awesome for words??

Now, while you and I were being challenged with a husband who wanted to control everything, we have friends who complain and tell us how their husbands are disinterested in anything and everything having to do with the home (and sometimes the children) and respond with "do whatever you want"! Why is that?

It is because God gives all of us exactly what we need!! For me, who was born with an independent spirit, I always wanted to make my own decisions. I always wanted to seek God and move in His direction without obstacles, but the obstacles are what make us strong! When there is an obstacle in my life, I must pray for wisdom, and patience, since I often have to wait, which strengthens me spiritually.

For other women, who are meek and indecisive, or maybe just need assurance, their husbands tell them to do whatever they want, which forces them to seek God for strength, boldness, and assurance.

All of us need God, so He gives us different ways to force us to seek Him *continually*! Isn't God good?!

Now that I am in the midst of humbling myself, which is always good to gain spiritually, a few of my problems were that I went to my ex-husband (when we were married) when I should have just gone to God. Some husbands who "appear" controlling are that way simply because we have gone to our husbands when we should have gone to the Lord. When I first learned about submission, I went to my husband for everything! Soon, I was feeling "oppressed" when the Lord opened my eyes to see that it was really my own fault. To add to this, I was raised with a mother who thrived, it seemed, on rebellion and sneakiness with my father.

Often, when things are out of balance in our youth, in the homes we grow up in, we tend to go to the other extreme, which is what I did. Certainly, not following in this pattern of keeping things from my spouse was a very good thing. However, one extreme can be just as bad as the other. How do you know when to ask your husband and when to just proceed with how the Lord is leading you? Pray. Pray and ask God to give you discernment. If He prompts you to ask your husband, then go and ask. If your husband stops your plan, then trust God to open the door if it is what you are really supposed to do; even when it comes to de-cluttering (what to keep and what to throw away).

If you are the timid type, who wants reassurance, and your husband has complained that you are too needy. Then seek God and stop going to your husband. If He tells you to do something, then go ahead with God's assurance.

For the married woman, her goal is to be able to live this verse in Proverbs 31:11: "**The heart of her husband trusts in her**, and he will have no lack of gain."

And how is this accomplished when it is so out of whack right now? With the next verse: "She does him good and not evil all the days of her life" (Prov. 31:12). Doing what is right, concerning your husband, begins with respecting and not challenging his authority, and extends to not speaking about him negatively with friends or family (not revealing his weaknesses in any area of his life). When you begin to be the wife he can "safely trust" in (that's from the KJV), then eventually he will allow you to make decisions without his permission. For me, the Lord simply removed my husband from my life in order for me to have Him as my authority. All those years of learning submission to my earthly husband has made me a much better wife to my Heavenly Husband!

Funnily, but when I originally revised this chapter, I wanted to do so without sharing my other faults, but the Lord had other plans. Another of my faults, which kept our marriage out of balance for years, was when I went to my husband to tell him my plan in order to get him to give me praise or a verbal pat on the back. I grew up with two parents, who unashamedly, thought I was wonderful and told me so almost daily! This was a good thing, but again if it is out of balance, which I guess it was, then trouble follows. The result was, that instead of getting praise, which is what I would have gotten from my parents, my ex-husband would find some fault or error in it.

This would also happen when I went to "bounce an idea off" my ex-husband. Dear sister, our girlfriends were created for this purpose! They love to hear each and every detail, but when you share your ideas, want to "just talk," or you need to "bounce the idea" off someone, for most men, it won't happen. A man would think that you want him to tell you what to do, not just to listen.

It took me a long time to learn this, but one day the Lord graciously removed my closest friends from my life, and then my husband—and I was left with only Him. Wow! What a difference!! Not only does the Lord love to hear every detail, He is honest when it isn't a good idea at all. And whenever He convicts me or shows me that it is not a good plan, He is so gentle and compassionate.

If you have the same problem of needing approval or acceptance, talk to God and ask Him to help you. There is no greater set-up for deep hurts. The enemy really has a hold on your life. People are the best tool that the devil has to manipulate and to hurt you. Look to God to fill your need of being loved, accepted, and honored. His spirit will fill you. No matter how many people you have praising you, you will feel empty. Just look at the celebrities' lives to see that praise from others will never fill that void in your life. Only God can fill it, so always run to Him.

Now, back to our chapter . . .

This method of de-cluttering and eliminating stuff (things that you do not need or use regularly) should be done throughout your home as you move through your house one drawer in one room, one at a time. Start in one designated room, and then continue to move through the entire house. Just spend a few minutes to an hour a day and soon you will be left with only what you need and use regularly.

Maintenance. Once you have the entire house: closets, shelves, and drawers cleaned (even your garage)—you can maintain this with the "clean sweep" method daily. The clean sweep is the exciting and life-changing chapter just ahead. But before you run ahead, remember, this book is a book of action. Reading it won't change your life; you will need to take action. So, take the next few days or weeks to de-clutter your home before reading any more of the book. This method will not only de-clutter your home, it will also de-clutter your mind, your spirit, and your life!

Chapter 3

Making the Most of

Your Steps

Clean Your "Messy House" in Minutes!

I will make a clean sweep of the house . . .
—1 Kings 14:10

I guarantee that this method will save you so much time, and give you such a boost, that you will never want to go back to the way you used to tidy or pick up your house. So often, we feel like we are picking up things all day long and still not getting anywhere. Though I still tidy when I go into a room, I do not spend my time or energy running back and forth to pick up or tidy my house, and I have used this method for years!

The "Clean Sweep" Saving Steps

This method is so good, it can even be used when you are lying on the couch with morning sickness, by using your toddlers and young children to pick up for you just before "Daddy gets home." I know from experience—I've done it hundreds of times! So if this method works when using toddlers or small children and a mom with morning sickness (who crawls from room-to-room and lies down on any available bed or couch in the room, or more often on the floor!), then you know that the "Clean Sweep" method will work for you, too! Here is my fool-proof method that is simple and yet works:

To Get Started

You will need: one to several laundry baskets for collecting stuff around the house (the bigger the mess, the more containers you will need), a trash bag for trash, and a large brown paper bag (or smaller baskets)—one for each room of your house for sorting.

With a black marker, label the bag or basket for sorting with the names of the rooms (i.e. "Master bedroom, laundry room, kitchen, Tyler's room, etc.). Save these at the end so that you can use them over and over and over again.

Clean Sweep

Gather. Now, use your laundry baskets, and pick up everything in each room that **doesn't belong** in *that* room. Begin in one room, and systematically work through the entire house. The best place to start is at the front door (or back door if your husband comes in that way). Put any stuff you find by the door in the basket, old newspapers in the trash bag, and any toys in the basket.

Tidy. Once you have picked up all the stuff (everything that doesn't belong in that room) and put it in the basket or trash, then pick up or straighten pillows, wipe down tables, make any unmade beds in each bedroom, then sweep or vacuum the room (by the way, *young* children love to vacuum). Your first room is now clean, so you're ready to move on to the next room!
Use this same method as you move from room to room. For me, it is easiest to begin in my room, then to move through the house in the same way. Whatever works for you; do it. If you seek the Lord, He will lead you to what will work best for you and your family.

Rules. Make sure that you NEVER put anything liquid or wet in the basket. Make sure you NEVER put Daddy's wallet, checkbook, or other important items in the basket. Instead, send a child (or go yourself) to put it on *his* dresser or on *his* home desk.

Confession: Years ago when I was still married, during an emergency clean sweep (see below), I put some of my husband's important items in the basket. Because it was an emergency, we didn't have time to sort the basket either. DAYS later (I had hidden the basket in our laundry room), when he was running out of the house, my husband had asked if I had seen his checkbook. I sent up a "flare prayer," and God brought the unsorted basket to my memory. I ran in, put my hand deep in all the "stuff," and pulled out the lost checkbook. God is good! Amen?

I don't think I need to give you an example of when something wet or liquid got into the basket. Even a "drop" from a finished coffee cup can cause you to have a real mess on your hands (see below for a *Tip* on coffee-to-go mugs).

Make sure that you and your children are completely clear with the "rules" *before* running ahead with this wonderful method. Like anything else, it can be a blessing or a curse, depending on your obedience to following the rules.

Tip: This is from when we used to live over an hour from our church, and some of us would bring a "to go" coffee. After I experienced what a mess "just a drop" would make, I developed this method that I taught to all my coffee drinkers. Once you have finished your coffee (or you pour it out), then put a napkin in the bottom of the cup and put the lid back on. This will soak up the "last drop" and eliminate a mess waiting to happen.

Sort. Once you have picked up each room, and then cleaned and tidied what remains in that room, bring all the baskets to one location.

Now, sort the collected "stuff" for each of your rooms: each bedroom, each bathroom, the kitchen, living room, laundry room, etc. When you have the items sorted, take that bag or small basket back to each room (that is already neat) and put the items away!

If you use young children, you would not want them to put the items away (since you may never find those items again). Instead, simply have them put the bag or basket right inside the door, until you can get there yourself (walking or crawling if you are suffering from morning sickness).

More Information on the Clean Sweep

Sidetracked! Do not get sidetracked by attempting to de-clutter a drawer or a closet (which you have learned about in Chapter 2). If you have not yet de-cluttered your house, I would highly recommend you set a specific time each day to do so (it will make keeping everything neat and clean extremely easy to achieve). Then, to maintain those "unseen areas" regularly, I have a fool-proof method in Chapter 7, "The Method" to assign them as one of your weekly or monthly cards.

Once again, do not become sidetracked. Instead, focus on finishing what you have started—"clean sweep the entire house!"

Handling Emergencies. If an emergency arises (like your husband arriving home early or unexpected guests show up), employ the "Clean Sweep," but wait until after things have calmed down or the guests have gone to sort the baskets. Just don't wait any longer—since you (or your husband) may not be able to find the checkbook, or something else you need, because it's at the bottom of a basket hidden in the closet! Once again, I know, because it's happened to me once too often!

Schedules and routines. Also, get yourself (and your children) on some sort of schedule or routine for doing the "Clean Sweep." If you are married, use your husband's schedule as a starting place. (We will talk about routines in more depth in an upcoming chapter.) But in case you are working through this book methodically, starting a schedule is simply to work into your life: waking times, sleeping times, eating times, schooling times, and cleaning times. Even babies are easier to care for, when you have encouraged them to eat and to sleep at regular times. (Though I do not promote the rigorous schedule of the book *Baby Wise,* I do believe in order and routines for children. See the lesson, "Your Mother's Teaching" in *A Wise Woman* for more information on why).

Keep moving. I once heard Elisabeth Elliot tell her listeners to just "do the next thing," whether it is doing the dishes or making the bed. Remember, "She looks well to the ways of her household and does not eat the bread of idleness" (Prov. 31:27). If the phone rings, or some other interruption occurs, stop and take care of it, but then get back to doing "the next thing." If you're the type that simply cannot get off the phone once you start, don't answer it, and use your voice mail to your advantage by returning calls when it is convenient for you (unless it is your husband calling). Talking on the phone has always been a major weakness of mine. Therefore, I NEVER answer our home telephone, and only answer my cell phone when it is one of my children calling or someone I know I should talk to right then. Otherwise, I wait and return calls when I am available, not any time anyone calls me.

How to Get More Done

Our main problem with getting a lot accomplished is stated in the following three verses:

"Her feet do not remain at home; she is now in the streets, now in the squares, and lurks by every corner" (Prov. 7:11–12).

"Let your foot rarely be in your neighbor's house, lest he become weary of you and hate you" (Prov. 25:17).

"I will set no worthless thing before my eyes" (Ps. 101:3).

1. Stay home more! *"Her feet do not remain at home; she is now in the streets, now in the squares, and lurks by every corner" (Prov. 7:11–12).* I know that if I find that I am unable to "keep up" with my home, then it is usually because I have been "out and about" too much. I need to look at my priorities and stay home, to bring peace and stability to my family. If you do have errands, try to do them all on one day each week that you set aside for running errands, as far as possible.

As soon as my oldest daughter started to drive, I began to have her do a lot of errands that I used to do. It was good for her to learn how to do the grocery shopping and how to return things. Even making a list of where she was to go on errand day is a valuable learning experience (which we will cover in an upcoming chapter).

Currently, I just wait until I have an appointment or have to go out, then I do as much as I can while I'm out. This keeps me at home where I find the most peace, and where I create stability for my children.

2. Stop talking to friends or family members on the phone. *"Let your foot rarely be in your neighbor's house, lest he become weary of you and hate you" (Prov. 25:17).* Whether you go visiting or call a friend (or family member) on the phone, if you do it too often, you and your friend will eventually become a nuisance to each other. Set a time to get together on a regular basis, rather than being "home in body" but continually "out to lunch" in your mind and your focus, while you are chitchatting on the phone.

You would be surprised that most of the distress in your life and home is caused by how often you neglect your home and children through telephone calls and other interruptions. I stopped accepting calls during my home school hours, because inevitably, it would cause me to lose control over the children. If they did "just keep working" as I asked them to do, they would do something wrong that had to be redone. You can always return calls to people who call at a more convenient time for you and your family. As I said, use the voice mail to your advantage, or ask an older child to screen your calls. Everyone will be happier for it!

Whether you are the one who calls, or the one who is called, the telephone (and now that cell phone) can be a tremendous curse on a well-run home or for a peaceful existence.

3. Turn it off! *"I will set no worthless thing (perfect example: your television set!) before my eyes" (Ps. 101:3).* To me, there is nothing more worthless than the TV. We used to have just one television that my husband plugged in on occasion to watch sports (that I would have loved to throw in the trash!) And we had one that was connected only to a VCR that was good for educational tapes, spiritual tapes, and for "family night" (when we watched a good black and white classic movie, ate pizza, and had candy for dessert on Fridays).

These were the "good old days!" God put me through another refining and "dying to myself" experience when we moved from our farm into the city. I had to learn a new level of submission; this time, with a more willing heart and to give a "cheerful" response when my husband (when I was still married) announced that we were getting "satellite television" (connecting our television set to the entire world!), a huge plasma (flat screen) television, along with another very large television for our living room!!

If you are trying to pressure your husband to remove the television, stop and pray; avoid the strife and trust God! (See "Won Without a Word" in *A Wise Woman*.)

Just for the record, I used to foolishly think that somehow, or in some way, I needed to make sure that my husband knew and understood my concerns and displeasure of things that I believed were worldly or evil. I was wrong. I realized that I had based my decision on my fear (never base anything on fear) that if I didn't tell him that I disapproved of having a television (or any other evil) that I would end up like Ananias and Sapphira (see Acts 5:1–11).

In the past, I was equally incorrect when I made sure that I told my husband of my displeasure of things he did, not because of fear, but because of my pride and spiritual arrogance. I believed my husband needed to be taught, by me, things that were right and wrong. This type of "mothering" your husband will end up in his tuning you out completely and not asking your opinion on *anything*. But true to type, a woman like myself either doesn't realize this or really doesn't care. We believe that it is *our responsibility* to lead our family if "he won't." Dear reader, there is no better way to drive your husband from the things of God and doing the right thing than to usurp your husband's position and authority. (To gain more information, get and read *A Wise Woman* because you are tearing down your own house!)

This time around, the Lord encouraged me to grow up; He showed me that HE knew my heart. He knew that I didn't want to have a television again after more than a dozen years of not having one. God always knew my heart, when I was faced with something I was concerned about and not wholeheartedly for. I didn't need to make sure my husband knew it! My job, as a respectful helpmeet, was to smile and to AGREE. Then I was to take my concerns to the Lord so that He could deal with it, if necessary. The self-righteous Pharisee always wants to come back, so I always needed to be careful to not judge what my husband (now my ex-husband) was or is doing or not doing.

In the last revised edition of *workers@home,* I shared that maybe it was **me** who needs to lighten up! But that if it were my husband who needed to see the danger in something that is coming in or going on in our home, then I could trust that God would bring it about while I stayed joyful, rather than being stressed or worried.

Ladies, give it all to God to work it out. Remember, "His yoke is easy and His burden is light"!

The reason that the Lord allowed this, and other things to come back into our home, and back into my husband's life, was because my husband (now my ex-husband) did not share my convictions at all. This meant that my children (even though I never voiced it) were living in a home where there was double-mindedness. God remedied this by giving my husband over to his pursuits (which were the things of this world), which led to him leaving and marrying another woman.

Though to some this may seem tragic, the truth is that God has blessed our family. Now our family's head is the Lord who is my Husband (Isa. 54:4–6) and my children's Father (Ps. 146:9). By allowing the wickedness to increase, rather than what I used to do by standing in the way with my opinions of displeasure, my children are now spiritually growing by leaps and bounds!

"A senseless man has no knowledge, nor does a stupid man understand this: That when the wicked sprouted up like grass and all who did iniquity flourished, it was only that they might be destroyed forevermore" (Ps. 92:6–8).

"How blessed is the man who does not walk in the counsel of the wicked, nor stand in the path [or way] of sinners..." (Ps. 1:1).

Though divorce would never be my choice, it was God's will that I might be an encouragement to women around the world to seek the

Lord for the Husband that all of us dream about. And you don't have to be unmarried to take Him as your own. (Please read *The Abundant Life* for more information on finding true and lasting joy!)

The *Morning* or *Evening* Clean Sweep

The "clean sweep" is a wonderful tool for getting your home ready before your husband comes home, or just to have a clean home to enjoy at the end of your day whether you are married or not. If you are married, or are expecting company, take just a few minutes to "clean sweep" your home, beginning at the front or back door and working toward the master bedroom or kitchen, whichever direction your husband or guests will take.

If your husband has a job that doesn't have set hours so that you don't always know when he is coming, ask him, if he can, to give you a quick call an hour, half an hour, or even fifteen minutes before he will arrive so that you will be ready for him.

Prior to training my children to do the clean sweep, before they were even old enough to help, I used the "clean sweep" method every morning. I believe that all women will find that doing this will help when starting or ending your day.

Here is what I used to do when my older two children were young: After we would all wave goodbye to daddy in the morning, I would immediately set out a set of toys for my children to occupy themselves (more about this in Chapter 9 "Toys") and then head upstairs for a *morning* "clean sweep." I would head to my room, make my bed, pick up or tidy around, and throw things that didn't belong in that room into a laundry basket, including dirty clothes or towels. Then I headed to the master bathroom, then the children's room. I would also empty the trash baskets into a brown bag that I would have with me.

If necessary and if the children were still quietly playing downstairs, I would give the upstairs rooms a quick vacuum. Then I would head downstairs, check on the children, and sort the "clean sweep" baskets in the laundry room. I would start a load of laundry, head to the kitchen to load the dishwasher, and wipe down the counters.

I also kept the upstairs rooms off limits, except for naptime, which is easy to do if you don't store toys in the children's room (once again, we will cover the toy dilemma in Chapter 9 "Toys"). Oh, while your children are young, because they seem to want to gravitate to the clean rooms, get a small gate to deter them from returning to clean areas of your house.

Those Who Work Outside the Home

All of us can benefit from this method of going from room-to-room, once a day, with a "clean sweep"— especially those of you who run off to work! This method will bless you, so that when you return home exhausted from a hard day at work—you will come home to a clean house.

For those of you who work, you can easily incorporate this routine either first thing in the morning (if you are a morning person) or just before you go to bed, which is what I do now even though I don't work outside my home.

A half an hour before going to bed, I clean sweep beginning in the kitchen, then onto the living room, before retiring each night. After years of doing this with my children, most of them do it themselves, and even do it for me when I have been too tired to do it myself (since I am now a single mom of six still living at home). Imagine my joy when I wake up and see it done for me! This verse is so true: "Train up a child in the way he should go, even when he is old he will not depart from it" (Prov. 22:6).

Ladies, with this kind of method set in your daily routine—you will feel absolutely wonderful! You will also find that doing it every morning, or every evening, helps your home stay clean and your life is less stressful.

Conclusion

Ladies, I guarantee that the "clean sweep" will revolutionize your life, and make your life joyful again. Rather than cleaning the way most of us have done, by running back and forth, and tidying messes on and off as you find them—you will do it systematically and routinely.

Once again, the "clean sweep" is simply taking a large laundry basket or two and beginning in one area of the house, picking everything up off the floors, tables, shelves, etc. as you "sweep" through the house. Once the house is completely clean, sort what you have collected into bags or baskets for each room.

And as I said earlier, I found that the easiest way to sort your baskets is to label brown paper shopping bags. Label one bag for each room in the house, and label another one for "trash" or bring the trashcan to where you are sorting. Sort and fill up the bags for each room. Once everything is sorted, take the bags to each room (that is now already clean) and put the items away. Save the bags by folding them, putting them all into one brown bag, and storing it in your laundry room next to your laundry baskets.

This method is, by far, the fastest way to clean a house, because it is so efficient in saving you so many steps! A tidy home keeps the stress down in the life of your family. I have used this method (and every method in this book) for years and have taught hundreds of women to do the same. I pray that it will be the answer to your prayer.

———— Chapter 4 ————

Your Day

Establishing a Routine

Instead, you ought to say,
'If the Lord wills,
we shall live and also do this or that.'
—James 4:15

Having a plan and setting a routine for going about your day is important in every home. With more outside activities, more children, or more responsibilities that you and/or your children have, an established routine becomes all the more necessary. If you set certain times for getting up, going to bed, meal times, and do the **same** tasks in the **same** order **every day**; you will spend less time to do just about everything, leaving you time to do more than you do now, or giving you time to simply relax. And when you have children, by having a well-defined routine, you will spend less time giving new directions, you will have well-trained and well-behaved children, and this will help them to accomplish much more every day.

She **rises!** Proverbs 31:15 tells us, "She rises while it is yet night, and gives food to her household and a portion to her maidens." Though the "Proverbs 31 woman" actually refers to the guidelines that a mother gave her son to find a precious wife, and it is not a measuring stick to see if we are making it as a wife, we can glean much from the wisdom that is found in these verses in Proverbs.

Just recently, we moved to a neighborhood, and one of our pastors lives around the corner. To my shock, my young children came home one day from visiting them to exclaim that they had a maid! Their mom is much younger than I am, with their oldest being the same age as my youngest child. When I went up to visit one day, I told her how from the first day I read the verse in Proverbs 31 about "giving a portion to her maidens," I had been praying and believing that some day I would have just one maid to wake up and feed! Now here she was with a maid, for whom she couldn't possibly have prayed for as long as I had!

After our lighthearted laughter, I told her that I guess the Lord is not going to give me one so that I can encourage women who also will never have one. If you are in the U.S.A., there is a good chance that you do not have domestic help, but I was surprised how many other women around the world are blessed with live-in or daily help (it makes me think of moving out of the country someday, especially when I have fewer little helpers, my children, who help to keep my home running well and cleaned from top to bottom. So God did give me the desires of my heart, lots of children, and I would rather have them around than any hired help.

As you read through this chapter, you may be saying, "Well, my children are too young to help" or "I only have two children." Firstly, I too, at one time, had only small, young children. Yet, I will tell you honestly that if you take the time by investing in their future (and yours), by training them to do whatever they can at a young age, you will reap great rewards later. By the time a child is walking, he or she can be encouraged to bring things to you and to put away their toys. If you invest time, effort, and your enthusiasm to get your children to "help" (even if it wouldn't take you a fraction of the time), each time your patience works for you, you are investing into both your futures.

Having said that, let me also explain that with a home that is de-cluttered and run well, if you have just a few children or if they are young, you will have less of a mess to deal with. In our home that topped out at nine (currently there are 6 children living at home), we have more dishes, more laundry, and more people to leave things lying around. But I also have that much more help to do everything if I take time to train them.

With young children who are trained properly with some sort of routine, you will find that there really is not that much mess other than their toys lying around—but I will touch on that method later which, if followed, will basically eliminate this mess from your life!

Establish bedtime routines for yourself and for your children; things that you do in the same way, in the same order, each and every night. Next, establish a routine for getting up. Pray about something that will make getting up worth the effort. A lot of adults wake to a nice hot cup of coffee, tea, or hot chocolate while reading their Bible and/or praying. While vacationing in Florida, for me, a freshly squeezed orange juice is a nice change. As I said, pray about something that will encourage you to jump out of bed (or at least not to keep hitting the snooze button) and do the same for your children. On Fridays, for as far back as I can remember, we have had "Sugar Cereal Day"— that's one day, at least, that my children don't sleep in or fail to jump out of bed!

If you leave for work, and/or your children leave for school, then create a routine for getting out of the door quickly and efficiently. Thinking and planning ahead, and then doing it religiously is what makes your life run smoothly. Variety is "the spice of life," but too much variety makes life too spicy and unbearable!

Routines

Every morning, I check my menu for the day that I have planned and written out the night before. I prepare breakfast and begin preparing or laying out the ingredients for lunch and dinner. However, previously when we lived so far from a grocery store, on a farm, most of our meat and other items were stored in one of our deep freezers. So if I waited, even until morning to check my menu, the meat would not be thawed, especially during the winter months. So that's when I began to check my menu the night before. However, the monthly menu is also in a later chapter, so for now, the time to decide, "What's for dinner?" needs to be right after dinner or no later than before you go to bed at night.

Let me take a detour here in our sample routines to teach you a couple of things that will help you. If you use frozen meat, make sure you work it into your routine to check your menu (basically, what you will have for meals the next day) the night before. If you use fresh meat, then making your meal plan must be made no later than first thing in the morning.

Don't do what most women do and wait until when you should be *making* dinner to figure out what you are going to have, only to find out that you are missing ingredients, and then run out to get that one ingredient (picking up a few more things that you don't need because you are hungry) only to have dinner late—again! Or worse, they run to get fast food. The statistics today show that Americans eat fast food for 40% of their meals, and this is the reason why this exact percentage of Americans are over-weight and unhealthy!! Even if you don't care about convenience, your family's health (or your health) is at stake when this is the routine in your home.

Instead of falling into this obese and unhealthy category, just begin right now by figuring out what you are having for dinner either in the morning, or even better, the night before (especially if you freeze your meats). In an upcoming chapter, I will help you to create a month's menu (not cook ahead for a month, but just a menu, so that you "know" what you are going to have and to "know" that you have the ingredients *before* you start making it) and a shopping list to match your menu. This small investment of your time, I promise, will radically change your life and take the dread out of meals and grocery shopping! Everything I do is simple. Each method just takes a small investment of your time, but lasts for years to create a smooth running home and life!! Now back to our routines.

After I check my menu, I write the menu for the day on a marker board for my family to view. I stopped doing this for a while, and then I realized that it helped me, as well as my family, to know what was on the menu. The reason I started doing it was to cut down on that question we moms hate to answer—"What's for dinner?" It also helps my daughters to know whether they will be making up some cookie batter for dessert, or baking bread. For me to write the next day's menu on the marker board is to stay ahead rather than fall behind. What a great feeling!

If you are a busy mom, you might want to use a crock-pot as much as you can, so that your dinner is ready on time. My neighbor who invited me to speak to all her friends and neighbors about meal planning, told me she is up to three crock-pot recipes a week. She is one of the moms I know who used to be part of that American culture of eating out as much as five nights a week!! In addition to eliminating the temptation to eat out, a crock-pot makes your house smell wonderful all day! I used to set the table for dinner after breakfast. Then we began home-schooling at the table, so I would set it after school. When we lived on the farm, we had a formal dining room; so, the table is set immediately after we ate dinner to be ready for the next day. Do whatever works for *your* family, and as your family changes, change your routine for setting the table.

The point to this principle is to set the table immediately after clearing the dinner dishes (as we do since we have a formal dining room), after your breakfast or lunch dishes, or after you finish home schooling if you home school at your table. Just don't wait until you are trying to get the meal prepared, as most people do, to clear and to set your table.

My best friend since eighth grade lives in a very tiny place with her husband and two children. Although I realize that it is very tiny, I could not believe that they just push "stuff" aside so that just one person can sit at the table. If your table is your "catch all," please just run out and get some sort of bucket or basket to house your junk while you eat a nice meal at the table. You and your family deserve to have a nice meal together, and that doesn't mean in front of the television!

Most young people, who come for dinner, comment on the fact that our family sits down and we eat most of our meals together. Our eating together didn't change after the divorce. In fact, what did change was the number of guests that we have over almost daily for dinner or for Saturday breakfast. When I found out that my husband was divorcing me again, I was determined to look for the blessings in everything and to take full advantage of each situation. Meals were one of them. My ex-husband was always concerned about money, but I know that God supplies ALL of our needs and He always encourages us to give! If you are having trouble with financial woes, then please read my book online *The Poverty Mentality*. If it is the divorce that is causing you trouble, read my book *Facing Divorce*. These are available for free online.

Food from afar. Currently, I "bring food from afar" once a week for my fresh ingredients, such as fruit, vegetables, meat, and dairy from a local grocery store. My major shopping is also done just once a week after I plan my meals for the month. When we lived on the farm (and were first blessed with a deep freezer), I shopped only once a month. Do whatever works for your situation and for your family. Make your fresh food and meal shopping part of your routine.

When we moved to our farm, almost all of our meat was raised on our land and butchered. We had several months of meat in our meat freezer to choose from and to work our menu around. The rest of our once-a-month shopping needs were done in "the big city" at Sam's, a discount warehouse, which was an hour away and "in town" at Wal-Mart, which was about half an hour away.

I tried several times to do all my shopping on one day, but not even our 15-passenger van could hold all the food with only one helper and me. I was also exhausted from two hours of driving, shopping, and then having to put it all away. After much prayer, I divided the shopping into two days once a month. We were also blessed with three pantries on our farm, but even if you don't have this blessing, you can store a lot in your garage where we store our overflow like paper products.

Then the cloud moved, and so did we! Now we live close to a city, just 5 minutes away from a huge super Wal-Mart and a 15-minutes drive to Sam's. We moved into a larger home, but it has a much smaller kitchen, and has no pantry. This meant that I had to revert back to shopping once a week, and for a while, my daughters did all the shopping for me!

My guess is that God wants many examples to make this book helpful to all of you, so He keeps the cloud moving in my life!

If you like to save money (or your husband has put you on a budget), shop at the discount bakery stores. There used to be several discount bakeries when we lived in Florida, and each had its own specialties.

So, ask around to see if these are available in your area.

You can also watch for a double-discounted day when you'll receive more savings. Most meat departments discount all their meats late at night and you can snatch them up very early the next morning (about 6 AM). Do not fear getting too little sleep—God only warns us about getting too much sleep! I used to plan early morning shopping once a month for meat. It was wonderful to slip out **all alone** since my husband was there with the children when they were small. Times have changed, now I am a single mom, but I still find shopping very early helps me to beat the crowd and allows me time alone that I enjoy so much.

Family meals. One of the most important tasks as a wife and/or mother is to prepare a nice evening meal that is not hurried or "fast food." It should be a time that the family looks forward to, and a time set aside each day to talk about the events of the day. Having a dessert, from a piece of fruit to a little mint to something bigger like pudding, cake, or home-made cookies, will help make your meals special. My ex-husband came from a line of Swedes, so dessert became a part of our meals.

Speaking of husbands, make sure that you are not trying to play "mother" with your husband's eating habits. Even if his doctor has given you strict orders, your husband is not your patient. I honestly would rather have lived with my husband peacefully and in submission to him (to reap the blessings of calling him lord, which I did, see 1 Peter 3:6 if you find this concept horrifying) for a short time, than to live a long and bitter life, which is what will happen if you usurp his authority! If his doctor, his parents, or his boss tries to push you to get above your husband's authority, smile and tell them that they are talking to the wrong person and to talk to your husband. *Now back to this lesson:*

To ensure a happy future, I incorporated "baking lessons" into my daughters' education. I taught my oldest daughter when she was about nine years old, and now her younger sisters do the baking. Baking is the best place to start when teaching your daughters or sons, before they learn to cook.

The men in our family LOVE having fresh, hot cookies or some other baked goodies for dessert! Our family is known for offering freshly-baked cookies when friends come for a visit. This is not how I grew up, but I am so glad that the Lord helped me to change so that this would be a part of my children's heritage and their own families as well once they marry.

Learning to bake (then cook) is wonderful training for your daughters' future. What husband wouldn't be happy with a wife who bakes from scratch! Truly, baking is a special and lost ministry to the church. When we lived on our farm, my daughter baked cookies and pies for many of the pastors in our church. Most of their wives did not bake, so it was a real treat and blessing for their entire family.

Look ahead! Once again, don't wait until four in the evening when everything is in a crazy state (when the house is a disaster and the baby is just waking up from his nap) to wonder, "What should we have for dinner?" Check your menu just after breakfast, but even better, the night before, especially if you plan to use frozen meat.

Make it easy! Plan your special big meals only occasionally. I only fix a hot, big breakfast on Saturdays for my family. My best recipes are in a later chapter; many have won blue ribbons but are *easy* to make. When we lived on the farm, it became necessary to fix a big, hot breakfast two to three other mornings during the week. But God is good—my oldest daughter loved to receive the praise of the family, and she would wake early just to make these extra hot meals for me!

Just remember, never be afraid of simplicity to balance your life. I use paper plates on color-coded plate holders for lunches—Oh yes, I believe in energy conservation—mine. And I do care about the environment: our home environment of peace and less strife! However, I also love to treat my family as guests by setting a beautiful table for all our dinners and for our big Saturday breakfast. My family is more special to me than guests and they know it by the way that I take the time to treat them especially well.

Who's First in the Home?

If you are currently married, please be sure to have the things that your husband has asked you to do at the top of your "To Do List" rather than at the bottom. (This will save a lot of anger or resentment on his side and a lot of hurt feelings on your side!) Our example, Sarah, even called Abraham lord! (See "Wives, Be Subject" in *A Wise Woman* if you have trouble with this concept!) Therefore, if you are currently married, make it your main goal to put your husband's request as top priority! Doing this trained me to put my new Husband at the top of my list and I am so blessed today!

What's the point? Well, many women tell me about their rebellious or disrespectful son or daughter whom they feel they have been cursed with. Normally, children are bred to be rebellious as a result of their parents who are rebellious to their authority. The awesomeness of God is that even though my ex-husband was rebellious, my children are not due to the respect that I gave my husband when I was married, and that now I give to my ex-husband (in a different way, of course) since he is still their father.

My goal is to be an example to all who are watching me, to be a witness of my love for my Lord and Savior, Jesus, who is now truly my Husband! This begins in the home, and even deeper, in my heart. How about you?

Conclusion

Establishing a routine in your life will keep your life running smoothly and efficiently, and will result in you having to do much less instruction and disciplining your children. Your stress level will fade into joy, which will accompany a happier home, children, and husband (if you are married). Take the time to establish a workable routine in your life!

If you are wondering how this will work in your life, with all the variables that go on each week, then the next chapter will give you some suggestions as I share some of my varied schedules with you that may give you ideas that will work for you!

—————— Chapter 5 ——————

Making the Most of

Each Day

How You Get Started!

In the beginning God created . . .
—Gen. 1:1

Whenever I speak to a younger woman, who is obviously overwhelmed with the task of homemaking, I quickly find certain distinct areas of neglect. The very first area of neglect very often is in creating a daily routine for her and her children, which we spoke about briefly in the previous chapter.

With that said, let me clarify my statement. I didn't say to set a routine for yourself, *your husband,* and your children—no, no. Do not think, suggest, or imply that your husband needs to be set into *your,* nor your children's, routine!! On the contrary, you and your children are to fit into *your husband's* routine.

"The heart of her husband trusts in her [his wife], and **he** *will have no lack of gain*" (Prov. 31:11). Can your husband trust that he will have no lack of gain?

"Then the Lord God said, 'It is not good for the man to be alone; I will make him a *helper suitable* **for him**'" (Gen. 2:18). If being a helper to your husband is a new concept to you, or if you are still struggling with this frame of mind, please read (or re-read) Lesson 9, "Helper Suitable," in *A Wise Woman* which is available through our ministry's online store. Go to RestoreMinistries.net for more information.

Now you might want to tell me that your husband's life has no rhyme or reason to it, but that is where you are wrong. All human beings are creatures of habit. If you think that your husband doesn't have a morning routine, I will tell you that you haven't been watching! Remember, "An excellent wife, who can find? For her worth is far above jewels" (Prov. 31:10). It was very difficult to find a virtuous woman back when Proverbs was written—now, it is nearly impossible!

So what caused a virtuous woman to be harder to find in today's world? The new feminist ideas have warped our minds, and now our thinking has become distorted. This verse of Scripture should set us straight. "For man does not originate from woman, but woman from man; for indeed man was not created for the woman's sake, but woman for the man's sake" (1 Cor. 11:8–9). This principle forms the very foundation of our homes. Without a godly foundation, our houses will fall as we unknowingly tear them down with our very own hands! "The wise woman *builds* her house, but the foolish *tears it down* with her *own* hands" (Prov. 14:1).

Once again, the very first step you must make is to set yourself and your children a **ROUTINE that is** adapted to your *husband's* schedule. You may think the terms "schedule" and "routine" are interchangeable, but they are not. A schedule denotes "time," whereas a routine is a pattern of carrying out certain activities. Now, certainly *time* will be a factor in your routine; however, I have found that when I use time to set my routine, I soon become stressed, anxious, and eventually frantic!

Once again, a routine is simply a way of carrying out your activities in a particular order, every day. Your present routine may be to get up, get coffee, yell at your children to "stop . . .!," then to sit down in front of the television to watch a morning show until lunch.

Or your routine may be to get up late, run to your children's room, yell "get up we're late!," throw cereal in a bowl, pitch something into their lunch box, and spend ten minutes in panic as you desperately search for homework, a shoe, or something else you can't find. Everyone has a routine. What I propose is that you establish your routine. Don't let it establish you.

When you set out with an idea for your routine, don't make it lofty and unattainable. How many times have you decided to take control of your day, and then you give up before lunch? You are not a failure if this has happened to you. You simply did not have the right mind-set when you began.

Wake Up

The first thing you'll do in the morning is to wake up, so let's begin there. Do you set an alarm, or do you rise when you hear your children fighting? Or, do you open one eye when your husband kisses you good-bye? Does he slip out hoping he won't have to confront your weary face, mangled hair, and offensive breath?

How would you *like* to begin your day? *Be careful and don't get lofty here, girls.* Set a time that you can easily (or at least might be able to) achieve. It may be nice to consider getting up ahead of, or at least when your husband gets up. Wouldn't you agree? Let me suggest that you go in and splash some warm or cool water on your face, maybe even brush your teeth. Do you like coffee, hot tea, or maybe juice in the morning? Even a nice, cool glass of water will help to get you going. Why not find out what your husband likes to drink, and bring it to him with a good morning kiss?

If it's also time for your children to get up, awaken them with a kiss, or a back rub if they are grown-up boys. My youngest daughter loves coffee (terrible, but true). When I sit down on her bed holding my cup of coffee, I offer her a sip, which brings a smile, a long stretch, and then she sits up.

If your children don't "have to" get up yet, let them sleep just a bit so that you can fulfill this wonderful proverbial suggestion: "She rises also while it is still night, and gives food to her household, and portions to her maidens" (Prov. 31:15). When I first read this, I thought, "Well, once I get some maidens (just one maid would be great), then I'll get up when it's still dark!" Years ago, the way I rationalized this verse was to tell myself that even though it wasn't dark outside, I *felt* like it was!

I know many women who do this sort of thing (get up when it's still dark). I just recently got a book from a woman who scheduled her entire day (every minute of every day) and individually scheduled her eight children's every minute too. When she sat down to write everything she needed to do every day, she found that she couldn't do it all in 24 hours! (I can relate!) So, she concluded that she could make it on less sleep! As soon as I read that, without even considering it for a moment, I said, "No way!"

Now, I will admit, I don't always get a nice eight hours of sleep, because things happen. Company may linger, too often we are out late on date night, we may (and usually do) stay up visiting with our older children, or there are times when a child is sick—but for heaven's sake, I am not going to *plan* to get less sleep on purpose!

I prefer to claim this Scripture to guide me in this all-important decision: "It is vain for you to rise up early, to retire late, to eat the bread of painful labors; for He gives to His beloved even in his sleep" (Ps. 127:2). Did you notice the verse said that we shouldn't "retire late"? I pad my designated bedtime by half an hour so I can get to bed at a decent hour every night whenever possible.

However, since I am getting older and after having lived on a farm, it has become more difficult to sleep in. I am often up at four or five in the morning. It makes me laugh to read the above paragraphs, with a little bit of longing for how things used to be! However, I never knew that I was missing the most beautiful sunrises, or the precious solitude of the morning hours spent with the Lord, until we moved to our farm. And even though we no longer live on a farm, God faithfully wakes me before dawn to spend time and coffee with Him!

Can't Get Up

If you have trouble (or you have trouble with your children) getting up, I have the solution. The problem is that most people do this backwards. They keep trying to go to bed earlier so they can get up in the morning. This will never work. Instead, get up (or get your children up) just one morning when you said you would—no matter when you went to bed. Then, don't take a nap (keep your children's regular nap short or miss it if they still take one) and then everyone will be begging to go to bed on time. Whenever you begin to go to bed late, which makes you get up too late, use this method to roll your sleep pattern back.

Are you a person who battles guilt because you feel that you should get up earlier? Are you the type of person who thinks that they should have at least an hour with the Lord—even if it means your "quiet time" would begin at 3:30 a.m.? Let me give you the verse that the Lord gave me when I was on the verge of a nervous breakdown (well, maybe my breakdown was in full swing when He gave it to me): "Come to Me, all who are weary and heavy-laden, and I will give you rest. Take My yoke upon you, and learn from Me, for I am gentle and humble in heart; and YOU SHALL FIND **REST** FOR YOUR SOULS. For **My** yoke is *easy*, and **My** load is *light*" (Matt. 11:28–30).

For almost six years, I barely slept. It began when my husband was gone, and I was seeking the Lord for marriage restoration. I just couldn't sleep because he wasn't beside me in bed. On many nights, I *thought* I heard him on the balcony of our townhouse. (I have always been a positive thinker!) I was sure that at any moment he was going to come to his senses and come bounding up the fence, onto the balcony, and tap gently on my sliding glass door. And, of course, I certainly didn't want to miss his coming home! (Read Song of Solomon 5:6 if you missed the picture.)

After he came home (which, by the way, was through a phone call, NOT through climbing up my townhouse balcony), I became almost obsessed with making sure I was the perfect wife. I had one baby after another. These three sweet babies would inevitably wake up to nurse, and I wouldn't be able to get back to sleep. I would go to my computer, and write until dawn. This went on for four years. The entire *Wise Woman* was written between the hours of three and seven in the morning and with one hand, as I nursed a baby at my breast!

Did you know that there is such a thing as "sleep deprivation"? Well, I had it. You get loony! Actually, it begins with becoming "wired." You can't sleep; you can't rest. Then you become loony tunes, and you're headed for a breakdown. It's taken me a long time to recover;

or have I recovered?

I am now convinced that we women have been duped to believe that we have to be super-human. We have believed the song "I am woman, I am strong . . ." But, that is a lie (I can attest to that!). The Bible says (and His Word is truth), "You husbands likewise, live with your wives in an understanding way, as with a **weaker vessel**, since she is a woman . . ." (1 Pet. 3:7).

Being weaker is nothing to be ashamed of; it's the way we were made. It was no mistake; it's not a flaw. God made us this way for a purpose—His purpose. And believe me when I tell you, whenever you try and change His purpose for your life, there's trouble.

So relax, get to bed early if you can, and get up at a reasonable hour. Now, we've spent over three pages on getting up. Let's see if we can get down to business.

Now You're Up!

Create your routine based on what you want to do, or what you need to do next. You will fall into one of two categories: the "need to do" or the "want to do" category. If your husband has not left for work, it is a "need to do." You *need to do* certain things as a wife.

If your children have a time by which they must leave for school, it's also a "need to do" decision. You *need to do* certain things as a mother.

I fall into the "want to do" category (praise the Lord). Neither my husband nor I go to work, and our children don't go to school.

(If you are interested in being set FREE from sending your children to school, you can find out about the BEST decision that my husband and I have ever made in the last lesson of *A Wise Woman,* and more specific information in *Enter by the Narrow Gate: Homeschooling with Conviction!*)

There is such freedom in living in the "want to do" category. If you are in this category because you still have only small children, and you are blessed to be at home—you have freedom! So hold onto it by keeping your children home and teaching them yourself.

Now, freedom is being free to do "not just what you *want*" but "what you *ought*." "For the flesh sets its desire against the Spirit, and the Spirit against the flesh; for these are in opposition to one another, so that you may not do the things that you please" (Gal. 5:17).

"Finally then, brethren, we request and exhort you in the Lord Jesus, that as you received from us instruction as to how you *ought to walk* and please God (just as you actually do walk), that you may excel still more" (1 Thess. 4:1).

Freedom that is ungoverned or not controlled is really bondage. Your flesh will begin to rule your life. You may even sit around in a lethargic stupor, as described in Scripture.

"How long will you lie down, O sluggard? When will you arise from your sleep?" (Prov. 6:9)

"As the door turns on its hinges, so does the sluggard on his bed" (Prov. 26:14).

"The desire of the sluggard puts him to death, for his [or her] hands refuse to work . . ." (Prov. 21:25).

Or, you are busy getting nowhere:

"She is boisterous and rebellious; her feet do not remain at home; she is now in the streets, now in the squares, and lurks by every corner" (Prov. 7:11–12).

"She does not ponder the path of life; her ways are unstable, she does not know it" (Prov. 5:6).

Do you run around from place to place, from project to project, from house to house, from store to store, and get nothing done in your home?

The second set of verses describe the adulterous woman. Have you been unfaithful to your husband, because you have neglected your responsibility as a homemaker, wife, and mother? This is why many men leave their wives, and why many young men are choosing *not* to marry. Why should they? Even the church is filled with harlots to sleep with. If he were to marry, would she be at home caring for their home and their children?

Would she be out working, while his children are raised in daycare? Would she see her responsibilities at home and with their children as her career, and work at it accordingly? Or would she simply stay at home, neglecting her duties?

Our older sons are now reaching the age to marry, and finding a "virtuous" wife almost seems impossible. A young woman who is not interested in a career is like finding a needle in a haystack! Even those who claim to want to be homemakers are going to college and seeking a degree to have something to "fall back on." Unfortunately, when you prepare for a "Plan B," it usually happens. (For more information on training young women versus young men, and more information on the dangers of being a working woman, read A *Wise Woman*.)

How long would your husband keep his job if he sat in the coffee room reading a magazine? How long would he keep his job if he went to run an errand for his boss and stayed out until dusk? How long would he keep his job if he didn't do his job?

Girls, don't come crying to me pretending that you didn't know. This is why men leave their wives. What man wants to come home to a woman with an attitude, who neglects her duties, yet has the nerve to tell him off?

Not too many years ago, men used to be frantic to find a wife and get married. A woman was a hot commodity, when her desire was to have children for her husband, train well-behaved children, keep a nice home, fix delicious meals, and be his lover at night. If this repulses you, then your mind is fixed on the evils of this world and you are ignorant of God's Word. If I'm wrong, then how did Proverbs 31 and Titus 2 get into the Bible?

Again I ask, have you been an unfaithful wife to your husband? If you have, repent before the Lord and ask Him to change you. Now that you're motivated, let's get back to the business at hand.

What's Next?

After you're up, the next step would be to get dressed, have breakfast, or make the beds. To make this decision, ask yourself, "What should I do?" if you're in the "need to do" category. If you are a "want to do," ask yourself, "What would make me feel motivated? What will keep me moving in order to conquer the next task? What will get me over the next hump?"

Some women feel a hundred times better if they can just get out of their bathrobe. Other women just need to get something in their stomachs, or to get their children fed. Some must make their beds before they leave their room to feel better. *If you are tempted to climb back into bed, I'd suggest you make up your bed first!* And some women like to walk or exercise.

If you are an exercise fanatic, let me first ask you a question. Once you exercise, are you so tired out that you can get nothing done? Or do you become invigorated and ready to tackle the world? We all know ourselves. Take a little time to ponder this question. *Selah.* (When you see this in your Bible, it means to ponder the thought in your mind for a while.)

Exercise is great if it helps you to stay calm, and puts you in a good mood without wearing you out. However, a good workout can also be accomplished by deep cleaning your house! Deep bending while picking up things off the floor, vigorous vacuuming to get your heart pumping, strengthening your arms by scrubbing toilets or bathtubs, or even making some good homemade bread with lots of kneading are all excellent forms of exercise. Women today neglect their homes and go to a gym or jog around the neighborhood. It's fine to keep in good shape, as long as your home does not reflect neglect.

To help you get a routine together, it might be helpful for me to tell you what I do when I get up, and maybe, a couple of other periods of time when I did it a different way. This may help you to decide how to set a routine for yourself.

Another Routine

When my children were small and not yet of school-age this was my routine. I would usually get up about the same time, seven in the morning, when I heard my husband in the shower. I would get up, make our bed, and tidy up the room. I would lay out my husband's clothes on his valet (that stand that holds men's clothing). At that time, I would iron everything as it came out of the wash and before I put it in the closet. But when our closets got smaller and cramped, I couldn't afford that much time to set aside for ironing. Instead, I began picking out his clothes and ironing them before, or during, his shower.

Let me assure you, my sons can all iron for themselves, and my daughters iron for themselves (the younger ones are too small yet, but they will learn). My daughters know that someday they will iron their husbands' clothing; therefore, often they bless their brothers by ironing their clothing.

After I laid out his clothes, I would go downstairs to make the coffee, sometimes reading my Bible, and waiting until I'd hear the little ones stirring upstairs. (When children have a set routine of eating and sleeping, they will get up at about the same time every morning.) Then, I would come up, kiss them good-morning, and help them to get dressed. By the time we would leave their bedroom, the beds would be made and the room would be tidy. And unless I had to clean the bathrooms that day, no one would go upstairs until naptime.

Then, we would all meet downstairs for breakfast with daddy and walk him out to the car, waving as he drove away. Once inside, we would go to the "locked" toy closet and pick up the designated toys for the day. (More information of how to organize children's toys is set out in Chapter 9 "Toys") Then, I would begin a load of laundry and check my chore cards (more about chore cards in an exciting upcoming chapter!) to see what I needed to do for the rest of the day.

One Final Routine Example

When I had four children, and my oldest had begun to attend kindergarten (I didn't begin home schooling until my oldest was just starting second grade), my routine looked like this.

My alarm would be set for 6:30 a.m.. I would get up and wake Dallas (Eeeeek, the infamous school bus!). I would go in and fix him breakfast, and he would join me in the kitchen after he had dressed for school. I would give him his lunch-box and backpack. When Dallas would come home from school, I would clean out his lunch-box, make his lunch for the next day, and put it in the refrigerator. He was taught to do his homework immediately when he got home, then I would check it; he would pack his backpack, and leave it by the front door.

Everyone else would be still sleeping, so I would walk Dallas to the bus-stop and wait for him to board the bus. Then, I would walk home, usually to find someone awake. I would then fix breakfast for the rest of the family, nurse the baby, and walk my husband to the door or to the car with the children in tow.

Once inside, I would again take out the day's toys for the children to play with. After they start to play with the toys, I would go into each of the bedrooms to make the beds, gather dirty clothes, dump trashcans, vacuum, and dust. Then, I would go to the next room and do the same thing. Ladies, it feels so good to have a clean house.

Another wonderful tip: I have never allowed my children to play in their rooms. Bedrooms are for sleeping, dressing, and reading. Sometimes, I have had play areas; usually it has been in the living room. And before they are ever able to go outside to play, stop for lunch, or lie down for a nap, the toys are all picked up. It's not difficult if there is only one toy bucket out at a time. (Again, we will get into more specifics about toys in an upcoming chapter.)

I really need to once again share my heart about home schooling. If you have EVER thought about home schooling your children, let me tell you that my husband and I believe it was the BEST decision we ever made, and this has brought about the good fruit in our children's lives that so many comment on.

I put together a video series and an audio series entitled, *Home Schooling for Him!! (Home schooling for the Lord that is and not how to get your husband to home school your children),* that will motivate you and give you the confidence to do it. I have simplified home schooling, put God at the center, and have shared this method with many women I know, or whom I've met, and also at home school conferences. They tell me that they now they find home schooling their children very easy and rewarding. Take a moment to go to our website store for more details—you'll find us at RestoreMinistries.net.

Conclusion

I hope that you can form a routine for your family from those that I have shared with you. When you make up a routine, then you need to *routinely* do it every weekday morning.

This is the place to start to get your life and home back in order. Variety is said to be the "spice of life." But too much variety (or spice) makes things wild and too hot to handle! If you don't have a routine, and you have to decide every day what to do next (not to mention getting your children to do something new every day), you will never want to get out of bed!

God is a God of order and routine. Every morning, the sun comes up in the east at the same time. Our seasons are set. Gestation of a baby, the labor and birth: all happen with specific timing and a set routine. This is God's way, a way of order and predictability. Become more godly by following His example and bring a workable routine into your family's life. It will bring the "peace that surpasses all understanding"!

———— Chapter 6 ————

Making the Most of Your

Schedule

Number Your Days

So teach us to number our days,
That we may present to Thee
a heart of wisdom.
—Ps. 90:12

Whenever I get excited with something new to try with my family, a crisis will never fail to happen. The enemy is a thief! Since you have prayed for help in your life, and God has answered you by giving you a new plan, then undoubtedly the enemy will come in to try to mess it up. Has this already happened the very first morning that you tried to set up a routine with your family?

The baby gets sick, your husband asks you to do something unusual for him, or your family decides to visit that same week. This is just part of every day life!

"Beloved, do not be surprised at the fiery trial among you, which comes upon you for your testing as though some strange thing has happened to you, but rejoice!" (1 Pet. 4:12) "Rejoice in the Lord always; again I say rejoice!" (Phil. 4:4) So rejoice! This just means that you are on the right track, because the enemy is trying to thwart your efforts!

It is always important to plan ahead, to set a routine in your life (as we discussed in the last chapter), and to organize your home and your life; but remember, tests, trials, and temptations will come into your life every day, so you must be ready with a plan of action—don't let trials take *you* by surprise!

When you wake up each and every morning, turn to God and ask Him for His plan. This is what the verse in Proverbs 3:6 means, "*In all your ways acknowledge Him,* and He will make your paths straight." This is especially true when a crisis hits. Go to God *first*, acknowledge that He wants to help you, and let Him direct the next step you take. That's how God can turn your trials into triumphs! And don't forget to **thank** Him for *every* trial, because He promises to work it for our good (See Romans 8:28).

First Corinthians 10:12–13 says, "No temptation has overtaken you but such is common to man; and God is faithful, who will not allow you to be tempted beyond what you are able, but with the temptation will *provide the way of escape* also, that you may be able to endure it . . ." We all face trials as homemakers, but what is important is to find God's way *through* it!

Methods of Organizing to Save Time *and* Frustration

Though the unexpected happens when you least expect it, we cannot focus on days like these. Setting aside dramatic events, let's focus on ways to organize our life so that when things happen, we will still be able to function or pick up where we left off.

Notes: Using and making notes are only good if you constantly refer to them, diligently follow them, and have the notes when you need them! Instead of notes spread all over your house, such as using "stickies," other scraps of paper, or lists, you may want to consider using an *organizer or appointment book* to keep your lists and all the other things that you need together.

Organizer: Organizers are wonderful, and I have used them for years. However, when you pick one, make sure it is simple and suited for your purpose. It seems as if they are designed for executives, and not for people like us; therefore, whatever you won't use, remove those sections and either throw them away or give them to charity. (I used to keep them, thinking that I would use them some day. Instead, they became just one more thing that led to my having to de-clutter my home sooner.) The best thing you can do is to keep only the sections that cover *your* needs.

When we moved to the farm and lived very far from everything, I found that I did not get out as much as I did when I lived in the city (when I relied heavily on my organizer that I carried with me everywhere).

This section was originally written when I was out of the house more often, which meant that I needed to keep my organization method *with* me. Most of you do not live in rural settings nor do you spend the majority of your time at home, so I want this chapter to minister to you.

The first thing you need to do with an organizer is keep it *with* you.

Even now that we live in the city again, I find that I try not to leave my home often, and if I do, it is for short durations. At home, I am constantly on my computer, which houses my "organizer" or daily calendar and office notifications, that remind me all day long of what I need to do and when it needs to be done. I also use my phone alarm to remind me of when things need to get done.

Though I clearly live in the "computer age" and on the fast track when I travel around the world, I have found that I really prefer the organizer method to a palm pilot. The rule of thumb is that you ought to use the method that works for you!

Once again, the most important rule when using any organizer is that you must keep it with you at **all** times! This means that you carry it with you when you move to another room in the house, and to make sure that your purse is large enough to accommodate your organizer as far as possible.

There are organizers that can actually accommodate my wallet or purse. Since I began to travel, I found that I have simplified my life and now I carry just a purse for bills, coins, and credit cards. If I do leave the house, it's usually for a short errand, and if it is for longer periods, I tend to carry my laptop to work on and so I have my organizer with me.

Another point: what works now, or what worked then, may need to be tweaked as your life and needs change.

Another great tip is to be sure to use a *pencil* instead of the *pen* that your organizer may come with. This goes for an appointment book or a wall calendar. Using a pencil will make it easier to move or to change things as events change, not only day-to-day, but sometimes moment-by-moment!

With an organizer (that I carry or one that is on my computer), I find that I am able to accomplish a lot more than I could without one and with much less stress! Here are some of the things that I keep in my organizer that help me to keep organized and on schedule.

Phone numbers: Okay, this used to be one of my best tips, but now, with the widespread use of cell phones and our SPEED dialing feature, most of this is passé. So let me just give you a couple of suggestions.

Make sure that you use your speed dialing feature for businesses you frequent and especially for your doctors or dentists (I love that I have this right in my hand when filling out forms). Key the number in for your bank, post office, library, Sam's Club, and your favorite take-out. The downside to cell phones is that I used to also have the hours these places were open in my organizer. Maybe there is a way in my phone, but I am not that cell phone savvy.

Calendar: Use the "monthly" calendar in your organizer if you usually have a minimal number of appointments (three to four appointments or practices a week). Or use the "week at a glance" if you are a fairly busy person (more than one appointment a day). If you are busy all day long, you will want to use a daily calendar or only use the daily calendar for those days when you're planning a lot of errands or appointments. I also like the hourly list for making lists.

I am a "stickie" kind of person; therefore, I seem to have them stashed everywhere so that I can jot things down when I need to. My method is to bring these and to stick them on my computer and transfer them to my computer when I 'm working on my computer. I also use them when I run my errands. The way to do it is to just write down everything you can think of, in no particular order. Just write each stop down on the stickie, and then *number the stickies* in the order that you need or want to go. Then I stick it to the dash board of my car and I never miss a stop or appointment.

Another helpful hint is to get into the habit of "scheduling" when you are to *leave* the house versus the appointment time. Just make sure that you write it down: "leave at 9," so that you don't get there half an hour early. Also, schedule the time you are to get ready and the time you are to eat (breakfast, lunch, or dinner). If you are a person who is always late, change this character flaw by padding your time. Allow 30 minutes, rather than 15 minutes.

Someone who is always late not only has a problem with being a disorganized person; he or she also has a problem with pride. What you are implying by your late arrival is that your time is more valuable than the person whom you force to wait for you each time you are late. Whether it's an appointment, a luncheon engagement, or at church—take time to redefine your life by allowing enough time to get ready and to get somewhere on time.

Being ahead, rather than behind, simply takes changing the way you plan things. It means no excuses. My mom, bless her heart, was often late by two hours! Her excuse was her 7 children; however, I also had 7 and was required to be early by my ex-husband. If he said we would leave at 7:30 AM it meant we were pulling out from the drive-way at 7:15 AM. We would arrive for church more than half an hour early and wait. And my ex-husband also did not believe that he had to help get the children ready or into the car. Ladies, I really had to seek the Lord for His help so that I was not a thorn in my husband's side and so must you. Even if you are not married, the children or your boss or your friend, whoever it may be, they want to know that you care about them enough to be on time.

Here is a list of some other information you may want to use in your organizer:

Children's section: Write the sizes of clothes and shoes, current height and weight, Social Security numbers, savings account numbers, birth-dates, blood types, and allergies next to your children's names. And always use a pencil! Periodically, update the information when you find that your child's size or weight has changed. You can remember to check height and weight regularly by using a green (or monthly) 3x5 card, which we will talk about it in the next chapter.

You may think that you can remember all this in your head, since you only have a couple of children. You may be able to, but what if, heaven forbid, you are incapacitated or should unexpectedly pass away. This information (and the method) would be invaluable to your husband and/or relatives like your mother or mother-in-law. Make sure that the people close to you know that you keep this type of data handy.

The weights are helpful especially with medicines. Though we basically *never* ever go to the doctor, I still like to have that information written down. You can also use this in your memory box by making a new card each time you update it (again, details are in the next chapter). Just remember to date it so that you remember when your children weighed that much.

For my husband, when I was married, I made up on the back of a brightly colored business card my children's names, birthdates, and Social Security numbers so that he didn't need to ask me when filling out paper work. He has kept it in his wallet for years—my children just told me he still does!

Husband's section: If you are married, don't forget to write your husband's clothing and shoe sizes, Social Security number, savings and checking account numbers, his co-workers' phone numbers, etc. Again, this is not only invaluable in an emergency, but it is also handy when you find some clothing on sale or if your mother-in-law wants to buy something for your husband on his birthday or for Christmas.

Addresses. When you use the address section of your organizer, once again, always write the addresses in pencil as our society is one that moves often. If you have a poor memory, you can keep track of a gift, for instance when it was received under each name (with the date) and when the "thank you"(TY) was mailed out. I began doing this because my mother-in-law would ask my husband if I got something from someone I really didn't know, and she would also ask if I had thanked them, but since they were names of people I didn't know, I couldn't remember. So after praying, the solution was to keep this information so that I could check and verify that I did indeed receive it and that a thank you card had been sent.

Also, make a note of Christmas cards (CC '07) received and the date mailed out for the same reason. When I get my Christmas cards, I keep the envelopes in a gift bag to check and to update my address book (that I now keep on my computer) soon after the holiday rush quietens down.

Prayer list. Record the date and the request, leaving space for the answer to prayer. Do you find that many people ask you to pray for them, and you say you will, but fail to keep your word? This is a place to write the request down so that we can be women of our word.

If it is a long-term prayer request, I make a 3x5 card and add it to the piles that we pray for during our family prayer meeting each morning. We have a specific stack *Pray for Others* that, **Praise the Lord,** have never gone unanswered. If it is a *Prayer for Salvation*, we put it in that stack of prayer cards and we often include a picture if we have one. Most missionaries have cards with their picture that we always use and add it to the *Praying for Missionaries* pile.

When my niece from Japan stayed with us and she was gloriously saved, it was so fun to show her the picture of her and her family that we had used for years to pray for everyday. She was just a young toddler and I was holding her. Prayer works, and so do these cards as a method to remember to faithfully pray.

However, since I am asked to pray about many things, I need to faithfully write it down in my organizer and then faithfully pray for the requests each morning.

Prayer tip. When I am approached with "would you pray about something . . ." I began taking their hands (unless it was a man) and praying right there and then! I stopped caring what people thought or where I was. I just thought, "Why wait to pray?" What is funny is that many of the people who always used to run after me to pray about something, stopped. Sometimes I believe that Christians like to have other people pray rather than praying themselves, or often, it is a form of complaining about what they are going through.

I really do love to pray and find it a privilege to do so; however, without a good method in place, like praying for them right then and there, adding it to my list in my organizer and then adding it to the 3x5 cards we pray over in the morning, it became a burden rather than a privilege. I hope one or all of these methods will help you to find the method that works for you!

Learn the secret of pre-planning. Make out your "**things to do**" for the next day, the night before! Use your organizer as a diary of things to remember, as well as what you are *to do*. So often, especially as I get older, I forget whether I did something or not. When I am careful to write my to-do list in my organizer and to check it off as I go, then I can refer to it if my memory fails me. This is especially helpful if your husband has asked you to do something! And make sure you put his requests as top priority.

Making your to do list the night before will:

- Help you to be one step ahead.
- Help you to sleep better.
- Help you remember if you already did something.
- And, if you are married, it will help you to be a better wife as you put your husband's requests on **top** of your list and treat them with "priority"!

The Correct Way to Make a List

The correct way of making a list is simple and it works! Most people try to make a list in order of what they need to do first. Yet with any type of writing (and thank God for computers), the way to write a book or a list is to get it out of your head and down on paper, and then to organize it.

Try this: when you make a list the night before, or anytime you are going to run errands, write down everything you can think of *as you think of it*. Then when your list is made, number them according to importance (remember, that if you are married, make sure you do your husband's request(s) first!).

If it is a list of errands to run, after you have written down everywhere you need to go, go back and look through the list for your first stop. It could be the closest location or the one that is the farthest away, and work your way back home. I taught this to my husband when I was married (not by teaching, but by example as I made lists for him) and also to my children, whom I do teach!

If you have a map, it might help to look for a route this way, especially if you do not have a good sense of direction. I have a map in my mind (though I, unfortunately, have absolutely no sense of time!) and looking at a map has helped me to find the shortest route to a location. I have found that the route that I normally take was clearly longer than what the map showed. Working with a map is also a wonderful thing to teach your children, whether you home school them or not.

If any of your stops are appointments that have a specific time, then I write the time, rather than the number, next to this. Then, I try to work my way to that part of town to hit the appointment time (padding an extra twenty or thirty minutes for me in case I get caught in traffic or get a slow cashier in a previous stop).

Unless I have less than three stops, whenever we get in the car, I write down each stop that we make in the order that I remember it on a little gadget that sticks to the front window of your car. You can find these little gems in the car section of your Wal-Mart. They have a pad of paper and a pen with suction cups to make it stick to your windshield. All of our cars have them. Recently I began using stickies and that works even better!

Once I list every stop, I then number them according to the first stop through to the last stop. When I was married, my husband simply loved this method, as he was usually the one driving. I loved it because I didn't want to tell him where we are going next! I never like hearing women always telling their husbands what to do. It makes for a bossy wife and a hen-pecked, bitter husband—not a good example for my daughters either!

Try this method yourself, and don't forget to teach it to your children.

─── Chapter 7 ───

Making the Most of

The Right Method

The Tasks in Hand

Let us examine and probe our ways,
And let us return to the LORD.
—Lam. 3:40

Most women have no real *plan* to keep their homes clean and orderly. They simply see a problem; then eventually, they get around to doing something about it (and sometimes they never do)! Yet, women of the past had a very organized manner of keeping their homes clean and in good order. It was something that they learned to do as a young lady.

The Method: Task/Chore Cards

When I was newly married, I had no idea how to have a routine to incorporate all the tasks of cleaning, laundry, cooking, shopping, ironing, etc. into my day, week, and month. I had never been trained nor observed it, as I mentioned early in the book.

You may or may not be in this desperate state, but very few manage a good home these days (as I have observed when I have visited homes). This method can either help you do what you have been unable to do, or bring you up to a higher level—all with just a little invested time.

Supplies: To get started, gather these items from an office supply store. You'll need:

1. One package each of white, blue, yellow, green, pink 3x5 cards.
2. A 3x5 card file.
3. 3 sets of dividers:
   a. Numbers 1-31 (to represent the days of the month).
   b. Monthly cards (Jan.–Dec.).
   c. And extra blank dividers.
4. Large colored paper clips or clothespins.
5. Plastic vertical letter holder.

What you are going to do is gather an ongoing "to do list" that, once made, can last for years! Each morning, my children and I begin our day by taking our stack of multicolored 3x5 cards that are clipped together and waiting in a letter folder. In the stack are multicolored cards indicating the frequency they are used. For instance, in our home we use blue for something done everyday, yellow for something that is done weekly, and green for something that is done monthly.

Why is this method better than a check off list or a chore bulletin board?

These methods may work, but the method that I have used since 1982 is something that you do not have to create over and over again. Not only does it last for years, it also is flexible. Chores or tasks can be moved from something you do, to something your child does, and then passed onto a younger sibling just by changing on initial on a card. This method is flexible since it can be done today, or saved until the following week if you or your child is sick or on vacation. I believe a method should not control you, but you should be able to be in control of your system.

It can easily be revised to do a task from daily to weekly, and it also has an easy method to follow-up to make sure the task or chore is done. Check off lists can work, but the downside is that you have to make new ones each time it is filled or you need to revise it.

So if you are ready, let's get started.

Getting Started. On the top white card you simply write each person's name with a reminder to pray to begin the day. With small children who cannot read, I have always drawn a stick figure of a little boy or girl on their knees, head bowed, and hands folded. Just to prove my point of the cards working for years, just last week I noticed that my 13-year-old son and 11-year-old daughter still had the little praying stick figure on their top card!

After each person prays, they put *that* card in the back of their stack and go to their next card, which might be to make the bed or a personal hygiene task (see below). My next card could be "Start the Laundry," while the children's could be "Listen to Bible Memory tape while making you bed." If your child goes to school, you may make a card "Bring your backpack to the front door," followed by "Have breakfast," and finally, "Get to the school bus—leave the house at 7:45."

The 3x5 cards are not just for chores, but incorporate everything you find you need to tell your children to do (or you make a list for yourself to do) on a daily, weekly or monthly basis.

To make it easier, each card is color-coded: blue is a daily chore, yellow is a weekly task, and green is a monthly duty. White (their prayer card) goes on top and pink card is the last card that says, "Done!" The daily goal or, better yet, daily *requirement* each day is to go through each task, one-by-one, until all the cards are done and the pick "done card" is on top!

Years ago, we called these cards "chore card." However, if I could make it stick, I would rather call them "task cards," since the definition of "chore" is an *unpleasant* task. I would rather that the things that we do to contribute to our family or take care of ourselves should not be thought of as *unpleasant*.

So, how do you get this stack of cards? First, once again, create a top card with the person's name on it to remember to begin your day with help from the Lord for *"apart from Me you can do nothing" (John 15:5). "In all your ways acknowledge Him, and He will make your paths straight" (Prov. 3:6)*. Either of these verses can also be on the top card as a reminder of who to lean on. Next, you begin with tasks that you do on a **daily** basis.

Blue Cards are *Daily* Tasks

As you go through your routine each day, write down each task that you do: this means anything *you* do or you *tell* your children to do on a *daily* basis. Write each task on a separate blue card. Everything you do on a *daily* basis will always be on a *blue* card.

Some things I do (or your children do) are out of habit; therefore, you do not need to make a card. However, I often write it down anyway so my children or I can organize our cards to learn to do them in a particular order. This is helpful when my routine is interrupted. I can easily see what I need to do *next* by referring to my cards. Some find checking off a task on a "to do list" is encouraging. This same invigorating feeling is accomplished when you put the cards you've done in behind your pink done card!

As I mentioned earlier, I began using this system for myself (when my children were just toddlers) so I could have some sort of method (without making daily to do lists or charts that needed to be changed or redone) to help me keep up with my household duties. Then when my children got old enough (about 5-years-old), that I began using the 3x5 card method with them so I wouldn't have to keep telling them the same things over and over and over again.

This 3x5 card method continues to free me up from having to spend my time getting my children to do what they need to do. This free time is accomplished by working not harder, but smarter and working more efficiently, rather than with more effort. This means you can do more in less time. With the extra time you can add more to your life, whether this is doing more or spending some time not doing anything—making time to relax. By following up and checking to see that their pink "done" card is up, I am also following up to make sure what I have asked my children to do is done.

Making Your Cards

I am the kind of person who loves making lists and organizing stuff. After speaking to many groups about my 3x5 card system, some brave souls told me quite frankly that they just couldn't do this sort of thing. So I had to ask God to help me create this method for everyone to use.

Well, God is always faithful! Soon I was just too busy with ministry to just "sit down" and think of anything. That is when the Lord showed me the easiest method for making the cards!!

I found the *easiest way* to make cards is to make the cards as you go. Each time you do something that you need to do, or you tell your children to do, then grab a card and write that task on it.

1. Decide *how often* the task needs to be done: daily, weekly, or monthly. Write the task on blue card for something you do daily, yellow if it's weekly and green if you do it monthly.

2. If you have children, determine *who could* do the task. Start at the youngest person in the family then work your way up; then, write their initial or name in the *upper right* corner of the card.

3. Determine *when* or what day of the week or month it needs to be done, and write that in the *upper left* corner of the card.

Let's get a bit more specific when making out a task card. On each card:

Write the person's initial in the upper *right* corner. I have two names that begin with the letter "T." So the older one gets a capital "T" and the younger one a lower case "t." (If all your names begin with the same letter, give each child a number according to their birth order.) My youngest daughter has a name that starts with "M," so my "Mom" cards are written out in cursive and my daughter's with a printed "M."

Blue *daily* cards are *always* kept in the paperclip or clothespin. The other colored cards (yellow and green that we will cover later) go in and out of the group of cards, but the blue *daily* cards *always* stay in the group.

How to designate who will do the job: I decide who is the youngest child capable of doing the job. (Always begin at the bottom, the youngest child available, and work up.) Most mothers start at the top and burn that oldest child out. And if they marry they will often choose to have few or no children. Tasks in our house begin at about four or five-years-old. Before that age, you spend far more energy getting them to do it and do it properly.

As you work your way up from the youngest to the oldest child, *you* will be left with the tasks that no one else is capable of doing. In addition, you will be the *initial* trainer and often the task supervisor (to make sure the job is done and done properly). Don't expect your children to do their jobs or do them well if you don't follow up.

This is also the beauty of this system. Each day, you need to put that day's cards in their stack when you notice the pink done card is on top. That tells you whether or not they *did* the task. Then in the beginning, and periodically, you should just take a look to make sure that they did the task adequately. The child may need more training. It may be that they are too young to manage the job, and it needs to be moved up to an older child or to you.

One of the most asked questions about my system is in regard to changing the jobs. My children keep their jobs for years! The only time they get rid of a chore is when I see I can delegate something **I do** to one of my children. When I pass my chore down, then I pass down one of their chores and so on. When a younger child is old enough for more responsibility, I look to the next child up, take some of their easier chores, and work my way up again to me!

When a job is passed down from one sibling to the next, the older child teaches the younger one to do it properly. The incentive to teach the younger sibling well is that the job doesn't come back to them! Often, I go over the job myself just to make sure that it is being done properly.

Now, with a great system like this that really works, you can see why I have no real jobs myself (and why I do believe that children are blessings)! If more mothers trained their children as they should be trained, you definitely would see *more* big families. However, most families keep their children as liabilities and not assets. They cater to them with outside activities, and wait on them like they are *their* servants. The children are not happy, but have an "attitude," and they are miserable. This carries into their marriage (a marriage that lasts less than a year), and they are home again. Mothers, take the time to train your children—everyone will be happier because you did!

Blue Cards are *Daily* Tasks

More than once a week and less than daily. When you have something that needs to be done twice a week, like Tuesdays and Thursdays, use a *blue* **card** and put "T & Th" in the *upper left* corner. If it needs to be done three times a week, like Monday, Wednesday, and Friday, then write "M, W, F" in the *upper left* corner of the card. When it is to be done every weekday I write "M-F" in the upper left corner. I like using a pencil when I choose the day and even the child, since it often needs to be changed.

I do switch jobs when they are not done properly. You may think that a child is capable of a task, but even after training it is not done adequately. Of course, when working with children, you need to lower your expectations a bit. But it is better to have them help (and maybe even come back in to perfect it a bit) than to neglect training your children.

Samples of Cards

Making your bed would be a blue card since it is done *every day*. However, if you or your child is trained to roll out of bed and make the bed, he, she, or you would not need a card for this task. However, since many homes have unmade beds day after day, more than likely this is a card that you will want to include in your cards.

Personal hygiene is another daily task that is often neglected by children. Sadly, it is often neglected by many mothers who are blessed to stay at home. Therefore, personal hygiene would be a 3x5 card you would want to add to your daily *blue* cards. Let me get off the subject of organization and focus on your appearance. Many unknowingly tear their own house down with the lack of care in their appearance. Husbands leave the house and are often met with women in the workplace who have showered, put on their make-up, and are wearing nice clothes, not a bathrobe.

Then, why are we shocked when our husbands come home one day to tell us that they have found someone else—9 times out of 10 it is in the workplace. For those of you whose husband does not work with good-looking women, they are everywhere when your husband leaves the house: where he eats lunch, the neighbor, or your best friend. Not only do these women look and smell better than you do when he leaves the house, but they are also very agreeable. They listen to your husband's frustrations, which are often about you, and she sympathizes. She may listen and share his dreams, like you used to do before you were married. But at some point, since your marriage, you have exchanged your enthusiasm for criticism as you tear your husband down.

Dear wife and/or mother, get yourself into a routine of looking your best *before* your husband leaves the house. If your husband is not in the home right now, start getting into this routine, and I guarantee God will bring him around to get a good look at you. However, beauty is only skin deep. "Charm is deceitful and **beauty** is **vain**, but a woman who fears the LORD, she shall be praised" (Prov. 31:30). So before you focus on cleaning up and beautifying the outside, you may want to get *A Wise Woman* and start on the inside. (These workbooks are available for FREE on our website).

Now back to our *daily* organization. Listed on this *blue* card for personal hygiene you might list what your child is to do, such as:

1. Get dressed.
2. Fix your hair.
3. Brush your teeth.
4. Put on deodorant for teens and preteens. (See chapter 15 for a great, non-toxic deodorant solution.)
5. And maybe conclude with: "Make your bed" rather than having a separate card.

Basically, you will make a card for each task that you normally are telling your children to do every morning, or a card for *you* that you need to include in your morning routine (so that you can organize your time better or to find your place when you are interrupted).

If you are a wife or mother who works outside your home, you will find that by using the cards (and training your children to use them to get ready in the morning), there will be much less chaos and stress. Your job will be first to train yourself to use them, adding to them as you see something you are doing so you don't forget, or adding something new with the time you are saving by working more efficiently. Even a card of checking on the children, or getting them up at a particular time (though I believe in alarm clocks for the children if you are constantly in a time crunch) will save you time and help your morning to run more smoothly.

Since I have delegated most of the household responsibilities to my children (though I used to do them *all myself* before I had children and also when my children were too young to help), when I was trying to give you examples of what I do each day to help you get started making your cards, I found I really had none to share!

Women often tell me that if they had as many helpers as I had they would be able to get their work done. Not really. It requires you to be organized, and do the work yourself before you can expect to move up to management. It wasn't until I had four little ones underfoot that I was able to even begin to delegate anything! And when you are teaching children, it really takes more effort and more time at first (which is why some mothers don't want to bother). However, your time, effort, and patience will reap great benefits for the future. I say jokingly (but honestly) that I could die and my home would still run smoothly because of this system.

Though I didn't die, I was able to travel around the world three times this past year—the longest was a five-week tour. I didn't have to do anything, not one thing, to get my home and children ready for me to leave them. The house was not exactly the way it is when I am there, but my ex-husband came for a visit and said that it was! Each of us sees things that no one else sees, but when you can fool an ex-husband, things have to be running well!

Whenever you discover a task that doesn't need to be done daily, then you will begin to make weekly cards, which are yellow.

Yellow Cards are *Weekly* Tasks

As you go through your daily routine, you will find that some things do not need to be done daily; therefore, you would do them on a weekly basis. Write each *weekly* chore on a separate *yellow* card. For example, "Dust the kitchen blinds" would be a yellow card if you do it once a week.

As you begin getting your life organized and your children are being trained to do what you used to run around telling them to do over and over again, you will then begin to see other things that need to get done, but just not as often. It may start out as a daily blue card, but you find that since it is being kept up, doing it only a few times a week is enough.

Earlier I mentioned using a blue card with M-W-F *or* T & Th, when the task needed to be done two to three times a week. This is the first step to modifying the chore to be done less often. The other variation is using a yellow card with just "Mon." in the top left corner, then another one for "Thurs." for instance. Do what works with your children and/or makes sense to you.

Since the yellow cards are not used every day, but only weekly, they are removed at the end of the day and put in the same day next week. For instance, today is Wednesday the 16th, so at the end of Wednesday, I will pull all the yellow cards from under each "done" card, and put them in my card file for next Wednesday right in front of the 23rd.

Each day when I get the family's cards ready, I pull the yellow weekly cards and green monthly cards. I then put them back into the 3x5 card file. Only the blue daily cards remain in the group.

For those tasks that only need to be done monthly, you would use green 3x5 cards.

Green Cards are *Monthly* Tasks

When you go through your daily and weekly routine and things become more organized, you will begin to see things that need to be done but daily and weekly is too often; therefore, you would write this kind of task on a green monthly card.

A good example is to clean off the top of your refrigerator. All of a sudden you notice that it is a mess, so since it has been like that for months, a green once-a-month card would be perfect. So I decide who should do it, have them do it, then make a card for that day. For instance, if this were the 20th then that would go up in the upper left corner of the green card.

Another example may be a changing-the-sheets green card. Though some families I know wash the sheets weekly, there are many homes where it is done once a month.

If you have a lot of beds like I do, try to space washing the sheets out over the month, doing one room at a time, and do it on a non-wash day. (I will explain more on ways to organize and simplify your washing in Chapter 13: "My Best Laundry Tips.")

To remind that room, I made a fluorescent 3x5 card with the instructions to "Change Your Sheets" and put it in my fifth child's cards the day before I will wash the sheets.

Tara then puts that fluorescent card in that person's room in front of their alarm clock. In the morning, that child (or I) do not make the bed, but strip the bed and put clean sheets on.

I keep a second set of sheets in a clear zipper bag (the ones that sheets, blankets and comforters come in). After the bed is made, the dirty sheets *and* the fluorescent card is put in the clear bag and brought to the laundry room. When the sheets are washed, they are put into the clear bag and put in that child's closet, and I put the fluorescent card into that same day of the month (For instance, if today were the 10th, then I would put it in front of the 10th to come up in one month).

To Sum Up My 3x5 Card System

The day of the week is always written in the upper *left* corner. Write the day the task is to be done on the blue *daily*, yellow *weekly*, or green *monthly* card.

Labeling: To designate which child, which day, and any other specification on each card, I offer the following suggestions:

Blue cards: On a **blue** *daily* **card** you may want the task done on M-F, or only Mon., Wed., Fri., or just Tues. & Thurs. Write this in the upper **left** corner.

Yellow cards: On your **yellow** *weekly* **card**, you would have any weekly task. Write Mon., Tues., **or** Wed. Write this in the upper **left** corner and keep this in the 3x5 card file holder in the next Mon., Tues., or whatever day of the week that job will be done next week.

Green cards: On a **green** *monthly* **card,** you would write the day of the month such as the 1st, 15th **or** 24th, etc. Write this in the upper **left** corner and keep this in the 3x5 card file holder in the day of the month: the 1st, 15th, 24th, or whatever day of the month that job will be done next month.

Once more: Begin by thinking about what you tell your children every morning, over and over again, beginning from when they wake up. Write what you usually say over and over on a *blue* card. If you have a chore list you've been using, write each task on a separate blue *daily* card.

For example: Make your bed and tidy your room would surely be on a blue *daily* card. Scrub the toilet or scrub the sink would probably be on a yellow *weekly* card. Wipe down the top of the refrigerator or clean out the junk drawer would probably be on a green *monthly* card.

Be specific: You can write out the explanation of how the task is to be done; i.e. under "get dressed," you would write "please check with Mom on what to wear" (if this is a problem you have with a particular child).

Can't read yet? If your children are too young to read, you can simply draw stick figures showing the task or cut out pictures in a magazine.

Can you explain what you do in more depth?

For weekly chores, I break them down into *easy* jobs. Instead of Tuesday—clean the bathrooms; write "Mon.—John clean the sinks," "Tues.—Bob clean the toilets (since he's the guy who always misses)," "Wed.—Tom scrub the bathtub (and do it after *your shower* while you're in it and still wet)," and "Thurs.—Cindy and Sue do the bathroom floors (the older one washes, the younger one dries), and Julie cleans the mirrors (she usually is looking in them anyway)."

Divide these jobs up among your children depending on their age and ability. Divide them up to spread out the work over the weekdays if you are a stay-at-home mom. For those who work outside the home, determine if this is a job that they can do when they get home from school. This makes just doing the sink, versus the entire bathroom, possible without having to do all the housework on Saturdays.

If you are doing the jobs yourself because your children have grown or because you are still waiting for God to bless you with children, then it is still wise to break down jobs. If you have more than one bathroom, do both of your toilets or all your sinks (include the kitchen) and all the floors on the same day. It is easier and quicker to do the same task in different locations rather than doing the toilets, the sink, the floor, and then the mirror. How do I know?

Years before the ministry, we owned a maid service in California. It was my job to train the women my husband hired. I trained them to do the same job (all the sinks or all the toilets) to help expedite their time at each home and when working with another maid.

Once-a-month or every-other-week jobs: Use a green *monthly* card. When I see something that needs to be done not once a week, but every other week, then I make a green *monthly* card such as "wipe finger prints off the doors throughout the house (toddler high)."

For **years** I had a green card for the boys' haircuts. Before making the card, I would wait until everyone started to really look shabby. But once I created this method of putting haircuts on a green *monthly* card, I was able to maintain that nice clean look by cutting my family's hair each month. My child training has paid off as now my third son cuts everyone's hair in the family except mine. I still cut and color my own hair, which has been very convenient now that I travel so often and for so long. I just carry scissors and hair color with me!

Each time I notice something unorganized or unclean (such as a particular closet or the refrigerator), I put it on a green *monthly* 3x5 card. When you make something that only needs to be done once a month, use a green card, put today's date (number only, i.e. the 16th) in the upper *left* corner. If it is a twice-a-month task add 14 days to the date (i.e., 16th plus two weeks, or 14 days, would be the 30th).

If a card falls on an inconvenient day (a weekend, birthday, or whatever), simply put it into the next convenient day. When you are filing it back in the card file, place it in front of the correct day listed at the top left corner of the card, not the day you finally did the task.

Another note. It is better to "maintain" cleanliness than to attack a disaster. If you wipe off the refrigerator shelves on Tuesday, and wipe the door (inside and out) on Friday, you will not have to completely clean your refrigerator each month. We eat all of our leftovers the day before I grocery shop. (Create your own food bar.) With all the food gone, I can easily wipe off these empty shelves to maintain cleanliness, rather than having to do a deep refrigerator cleaning as often. This is also when I sort chips, breads, and desserts. Anything that is not eaten is thrown away, or was given to our animals when we lived on our farm, and now to my oldest son who loves to be able to keep working since he has something he can heat up in the microwave.

How to use your Card File and the System

As I mentioned when we began, each family member who is participating in this system has a pile of blue daily cards that is held together with a clothespin or large colored paper clip. Each child (and you) has a different colored paperclip to help identify their pile easily. Or, you can use colored clothespins, or write their name on the wooden clip. (Since I use my same cards *for years*, the paperclips began to wear out the top of the cards. That's when I began using the clothespins.)

Every morning. First thing each morning (or the night before) look at the initials and lay the piles of blue *daily* cards (that are held together with a clip) across your kitchen counter or desk, from left to right— oldest to youngest member of your family.

Then, get the yellow *weekly* and green *monthly* cards that will be in the front of your card file with today's date (for instance, the 14th). In your card file, today's date would be in front with all the yellow *weekly* cards and green *monthly* cards that you pass out to each family member. In other words, if today is the 24th, that group of yellow and green cards will be in front of number 24. You will take them out and put them into each pile of blue *daily* cards (that are held together with a clip).

In front of the pile of each person's blue *daily* cards, you should have a **white** or fluorescent card with their name on it. This, we use as a prayer card that lists requests, which might include their friends' and family's salvation. Or, you can write out a card with a short prayer for that child to begin their day. With my daughters, I write out the verse about having a "gentle and quiet spirit, which is precious in the sight of God" that has helped their contentious ways!

The last card is **pink** and has the word "done" written on it. Once they begin with prayer, they begin the task on the card, and then when complete, they move it to the back behind the "pink done" card. The cards are NOT held together with a ring or made from spiral held 3x5 cards, so that they can easily be moved around based either on priority or by time restraints. (For instance, if there is a card to bring the trash cans in, and it needs to be done later in the afternoon.)

Pink cards. I use one pink card to indicate the stack "done" and pink cards are also used for birthdays (we cover this in more depth in Chapter 8 "Planning Ahead"). And finally, I use just one pink card that says "move next month's cards forward" that is set for the 25th of the month (written in the **upper** _left_ corner of the card). Put this card in front of the 25th card divider. Again, we will cover this in more depth in the next chapter.

One more time. Each person has a stack of cards held together with a clip. The top card is the white prayer card, followed by the _blue_ daily cards. Next are the yellow _weekly_ cards and green _monthly_ cards; lastly the pink "done" card.

Rules for keeping them together: Keep a special container to hold the clipped-together cards. All cards must stay there; no one is allowed to carry their cards around. My children's cards are in an old plastic mail holder.

Teaching them the method. Tell the children that as they finish a task, the card is put behind the pink card. After they pray, they work through each card. You may tell them they must complete each task in the order in which you put the cards (to learn obedience), or you may allow them to do the tasks in any order (to teach organization). It is important, however, that you do have a time that they are expected to have the tasks completed. It could be by noon, by 3 p.m., before they go outside to play, before dinner, or by morning. _However, do not say to do the tasks before they go to bed_, or you will have the latest bedtime ever!

My children got in the habit of taking all afternoon, instead of the hour it should have taken. So I began using a kitchen timer and set it for 60 minutes to teach them diligence. It worked! So this is now the way I set it up every day. Our children do their cards immediately after they finish their schoolwork. If a particular day clearly has more chores that have been "proven" to take longer than 60 minutes, you can easily add another 10 or 15 minutes for that one child to complete their cards.

Making it work. The method *only works* if you put out the cards every (weekday) morning, and you enforce punishment if the tasks are not done. Periodic inspections are important to see if they are doing their tasks correctly and thoroughly! Also, if you make them do it over for being too lazy to do it right the first time, it will speak volumes to that child and all the other children who witness that you mean what you say! In addition, if they ever put a card that is *incomplete* or just not done behind the pink "done" card, it is a **lie**! Punish lying severely. A **liar** is an abomination to God!

Special circumstances. Because you have all your household tasks on 3x5 cards, you can easily move any card to any particular day. If you're having company and you want the floors washed the day before your guests arrive, you could move that card to that day. If you find that during the summer you need to vacuum more often, you can make more vacuum cards; then at the end of the summer, throw them away. The most important thing to remember is that you want to maintain cleanliness, rather than always waiting until there is a giant mess. Use bibs for children and aprons for you and your little helpers. You have a very important job to do—so let the Lord be your boss!

Keeping "unseen areas" clean. To keep your closets or drawers clean and not become sidetracked during your clean sweep, you will want to make a "monthly" or green 3x5 card for these closets and drawers. The best method is to start doing it on a monthly basis, and later change it to bimonthly (two green cards spaced two weeks apart; i.e., 1st & 15th or 14th & 28th).

You will know how often you need to clean and sort depending on the severity when your card comes up! And if you are faithful to include your children in cleaning, you will find that they are much more interested in keeping it that way so they don't have to deep clean as often! In addition, if you are doing it yourself, it is much easier to keep a closet or drawer clean, rather than to let it get so messy that you need to clear out the entire closet or drawer as you did back when you de-cluttered your home initially!

Miscellaneous Tips:

- Use birthday (or any occasion) paper tablecloths for wrapping huge presents. I find tablecloths marked down at grocery stores and at dollar stores.

- Colds can be avoided or attacked with Vitamin C crystals. The bottle I have is 16 oz. for $28. When we hear of colds going around our circle of friends or our church, I add two heaping teaspoons to our juice pitcher. The older children drink the most, down to the youngest. At the first sign of a cold in any of my children, or myself, I make up a sport's cup with a lid (put their initials on it so no one else drinks from it), and I add one teaspoon to juice. They nurse on that throughout the day; and if we've caught it in time, they won't get the cold or flu. If we haven't, I repeat it for the next few days and it is over faster. Too much Vitamin C can cause diarrhea, but to avoid a cold spreading through eight of us, that's a small price to pay. In addition, we read on the Internet that if you do get a cold, take about 3000 mg every few hours to lessen your symptoms by almost 80%, and found that they are absolutely correct! Again, you may experience diarrhea when you take too much, but then simply cut back a bit.

Chapter 8

Making the Most of

Planning Ahead

More Ways to Use the 3x5 Card System

The mind of man plans his way,
But the LORD directs his steps.
—Prov. 16:9

As I began having more children, it became necessary to get more organized. I have listed a few more ways below to use the 3x5 card system to organize your life.

Get ready: When you are planning to go somewhere with children, you exert a lot of mental energy trying to think of what you need to bring. I came to realize that if I made a permanent list on a 3x5 card, I could write additional items I had missed each time so that I would have them written down for the next time. I could also erase what I really didn't need to bring.

I took a blank divider and made a "Get Ready—Go!" file where I keep all of these permanent lists that I "add to" rather than making new lists. Below are a few suggestions:

Diaper bag: Write down what you *must* have: how many diapers, a sipper cup, wipes (I keep two wash cloths in a sandwich bag for sticky hands or a messy diaper instead of wipes that are safer), a couple of toys, training pants for the toddler, and clean bibs. After each outing, I restock my diaper bag as soon as I get home so that it is ready to go (by checking my diaper bag card with the contents listed). This is a job that I began to delegate to my older children when the last three were born.

Purse: My mom used to carry everything in her handbag (it was the size of a suitcase) and she would only clean it out annually. As for me, I like to sort my purse once a week. I have a "sort purse" card in my "Get Ready" file. To properly "clean out" anything, you need to first take everything out. Remove all the trash, make a pile of what needs to be "put away" elsewhere and then put the things you need back into your purse. Next, check your 3x5 card list to see if there are things you need to restock, and add any "new item" that you may need to add to your list (or erase from your list any item that you no longer need to carry in your purse). Though I like to do this weekly, you may only need to do this monthly.

Tip: I carry a small scissors in my purse at all times. I cut threads that I see on my husband's or children's clothing, and even tags off of my purchases. But the really great way to use the scissors carried in your purse is for cutting up meat or pizza for your little ones when they are young. It's impossible to cut with the plastic knives at fast food restaurants. Surprisingly, it is easier to cut steak, chicken, pizza, and just about anything else, with scissors than it is to cut with even a steak knife. I bought the bright handled ones with the blunt tip (the good variety that cut well), and I find that this one item is used and borrowed more than just about anything in my purse. Of course, after using your scissors to cut up food items, you must make sure that you clean it well before storing it in your purse again. And for obvious reasons, never use any rusty scissors for cutting up food.

Couple "Getaway." Once, my husband surprised me with the exciting news that he was taking me on a weekend "getaway." (We're pretty sure number seven was the "fruit" of this getaway!) He said, "Just throw a few things in a bag!" My head was spinning since I had to get six children situated (well, need I explain?). I did throw a "few" things in a bag—too few! I had **nothing** to wear to bed—of course my husband was delighted. I didn't wash my face for two days since I forgot my cleansers, and he looked very GQ by wearing no socks with his dress shoes. I learned my lesson.

When I got home, I made a list of all that I *wished* I had brought that weekend, and made a 3x5 card labeled "Couple Getaway." Later, I added a "Couple Getaway with Baby" card, since my husband would often on the spur of the moment suggest a getaway when I had a nursing baby.

Emergency bags. Even if you have a well-stocked diaper bag, it's no good when it's back home. So I got a plastic container for each car and filled it with emergency diapers, bibs, a receiving blanket (this comes in handy for many things), and underpants for those who still have an occasional accident. I also carry a brush, comb, and deodorant (for the sweaty teens)! Of course, I made a corresponding 3x5 card marked "Emergency Bag" for each car. Be sure to include a flashlight, flares, etc. Don't forget the "throw-away" camera for recording an accident or a special event that you would have otherwise missed. They're cheap and can easily be replaced.

Special trips. Each year, we take a trip up to a river and stay in a cabin. Without a doubt, many things are forgotten, which makes it really "roughing it." I have two cards that are paper-clipped together that list everything that we need. Each year, I update and add to it immediately after unpacking.

On one card, I wrote what each child was to pack in his or her own bag. I wrote how many pairs of pants, shirts, underwear, socks, also a sweatshirt, P.J.s, etc. Under toiletries, I sorted them into categories such as hair care (brush, combs, elastics, hats, gel, or hair spray), eye care (contacts, glasses, or sunglasses), body care (deodorant, sunscreen, etc.), face care (make-up bag, acne stuff, etc.). The four oldest (I let them do their own when they are 10 years of age and upwards) gather their own belongings, while I pack for the three younger children. They lay everything out on their bed, and I check to make sure that they have done a good job (don't let them pack their bags first since it makes it harder to see what they pack).

For years, their suitcase was just a pillowcase! Everyone had a different color, and it really worked well. (Of course with our large family, we never flew anywhere. Come to think of it, we did use army duffel bags when we flew—when we had four children.) Last year, each of the older children got a nylon sports bag for swim team that we now use for trips. I bought each of the younger ones a backpack for their birthday. (Do not use these bags for the beach—sand will forever be part of your belongings!)

Now that money is not an issue, we have been able to purchase sets of suitcases that have wheels. We purchased the ones for the three younger children, and the older ones purchased their own. This became a "must-have" when we began going to resorts instead of to a cabin and when we began to fly with our children. Everyone is in a different phase in his or her life; do whatever fits your lifestyle.

Out to eat: When we *all* go out, we are stared at enough without everyone watching me try to figure out what each child wants on their baked potato! At most restaurants or fast food places, you will find, as we did, that everyone has their favorite food that they like to order, so why not write it down? I started by making out a 3x5 card for my mother, who liked to take the children out to dinner, to expedite things for her. After that, I kept the card with my money (bills) in my wallet. Then I began making one for each place where we ate out at. I even wrote down the amount that it cost, which helped me to see if I had enough money with me (before we charged everything to gain "frequent flier miles"). An added benefit was that I knew whether they had over-charged me! And if you are using a coupon and paper-clip it to your 3x5 card, you'll remember to use it!

For those of you who just let your children "choose" what they want, even if you can afford it, this does make for impolite children. Most children who come with us are indignant when I tell them they must choose "one" thing from the "dollar" menu when they have always ordered whatever they wanted. And when they are allowed to order, they often choose unwisely and order too much. Then they will either leave so much uneaten food or over-eat.

Young girls should be trained to be "frugal" with their choices, since most married couples are on a tight budget. Also, the young men need to learn how to be prudent in their choices, since they will have a family to care for. We all know that it is "easy" to learn how to spend money, but it is difficult to learn how to get along with meager means; therefore, a child should be trained to do so.

"Not that I speak from want, for I have learned to be content in whatever circumstances I am. I know how to get along with humble means, and I also know how to live in prosperity; in any and every circumstance I have learned the secret of being filled and going hungry, both of having abundance and suffering need" (Phil. 4:11–12).

Books. I tend to borrow and lend out a lot of books, and it is extremely hard to keep track of them when they are gone. So now when I lend or borrow a book, I write on a white card: "Borrowed from Sue" (or borrowed from the library) or "Lent to Sue" and the date I lent it out or borrowed it. I then put the card in my dated file to come up when the book is due at the library or a month later to *give* the book back or to *ask for* the book back from a friend.

When I return a book, I draw a line through it and write, "returned" with the date, but I keep the card for a while! Many times there might be a question by the lender or in your own mind whether the book was returned.

I also list on another card recommended books that I can't buy right now, and I use this card when someone asks me what I might like for a gift. I keep the card in the month of my birthday or in December's section for Christmas gifts.

When I read a book, especially a borrowed book, I write notes on a 3x5 card as a future reference. All of these are kept on a blank file card labeled "Books" that I keep in my file near the back (behind the days of the month 1–31 and the months January through December).

Birthdays! In the month section (January–December), I have a *pink* 3x5 card for birthdays. The name of the month is at the top of the card. Listed next is the *day* of the month followed by the person's name and the year (i.e. '78). Next, I put "send" with enough time for it to reach the person on time. The mail time is shorter if it is just a card; it is longer for a package.

For example, I write under January "7th Maura 1958, send card on the 1st.") When I hear that a new baby is born into the family, I write the day at the bottom of that month's card; along with the name, the year, and when to send the card (or gift) for their 1st birthday!

The pink card is pulled on the 25th, so you have a few days to buy the card or gift and mail it. (If it is on the first of the month, it may be wise to put it on the 3x5 card for the month before, especially if you usually mail a gift to that person).

I keep this month's pink card in my paper-clip every day until I have bought the card or gift for every birthday that month. Then, I put the pink card into the day the next card, or gift, is to be sent. At the end of the month, I put the card into the month where it belongs.

For instance, after I send Maura's card on the first, then I put the card in front of the 5th when I would need to send Jim's birthday card since his birthday is on the 9th of the month.

Tip: If you're like me, you like to buy ahead for birthdays and Christmas when you find a bargain or something you know that they would really like. However, many of us have trouble finding *where* we have hidden it. On a white 3x5 card, write out whom the gift is for, what the gift is, and where you hid it. Put it BEHIND the pink birthday card for that month. You will be alerted as to what you have bought and where you have hidden it on the 25th of the previous month. It really works!

Parties or other engagements: There is nothing worse for women than to wear the same dress around the same people, because you can't remember what you wore last time. (Does this happen to you, or am I getting old?) What I do to remember when I speak somewhere is to write on a card the date that I am asked to speak and what I plan to wear in pencil. I put this card by the date (or the day before) I'm scheduled to speak. When I put that card back, I write what I did eventually wear so I know not to wear it again. (If I don't have another speaking engagement scheduled, then I store this card in "Get Ready—Go!" section of the file.) If there is a date, then I put it by the day of my next engagement.

You can use this method for church clothes, business dinners, or even PTA meetings (though these probably call for very casual dress now, so it wouldn't matter).

Bathroom linen closet: In our first house after our restoration, we had just one bathroom with only one small cupboard where I could keep toiletries, medicines, bandages, etc.. It was almost impossible to find anything until I used my 3x5 card system. I first saved a bunch of the plastic gallon ice cream buckets with lids to sort and store the stuff. I numbered each bucket and wrote out a corresponding 3x5 card. I listed the number of the bucket, the contents, and its location (which of the three shelves it was on) onto each card. This can be stored in the back of your card file with a divider marked "bathroom" or in the cupboard itself on a hook. When you, your children, or your husband need something, just flip through the cards to find out which bucket the item is located and on what shelf.

This system came in handy when I was sick in bed or nursing a baby. My husband or children would bring me the cards, and then go and bring the bucket so I could find the item for them! Then a few hours later, I would ask for the box of band-aids or anti-itch cream so I could get it back in the bucket and send it back with them to put on the shelf. Though we have many more bathrooms and lots of shelves, this method proved to be more efficient than what we have now!

Home videos. When we got a video camera, I was thrilled. But locating an event we wanted to watch was frustrating. So one day, we (the children and I) sat down to watch all our videos "for fun" and so I could document the main events of the video on a *white* 3x5 card. I numbered the tapes 1–10 and numbered a corresponding 3x5 card. If I knew the date of the event we were watching, I wrote it down (or often tried to guess the date), followed by the event (like Axel's 10th birthday, Macy's first steps, A & E soccer awards, 1998 vacation in Ft. Walton Beach). Unfortunately, I didn't know that there was a button that marks the date on the film for the first couple of years we owned our own camera. With this method, we can now find anything we want to watch.

This method came in handy after my father passed away, and we were able to go back and watch the times we had spent with him. I hope to splice these all together, put them on one tape, and give it to my brothers and sisters for Christmas *some* year.

Tip: We made a tape of an interview with Great Grandma Brown a few years before she died. She dressed up in one of her church dresses, and we gave her a corsage. My husband, her grandson, wore his tuxedo from the church band. We followed the format of the "Tonight Show" as my husband introduced her and asked her questions about her life.

At one point, we (supposedly) turned off the camera to take a break—but we had actually taped it without Grandma's knowledge. With the camera off, she began to "let her hair" down and was less formal. That's when she began saying things that she wouldn't have said with the camera on, which made us laugh so hard that we were just about hysterical.

When we heard she had died, we made a copy and sent it up to Minnesota. The family later gathered at her home and played it after the funeral. They called to say that they had laughed until they cried. They said that it helped them to remember how she used to be before she got sick; they said it was wonderful! We did the same thing with my father, and it was also a real blessing. By the way, Grandma's was taken with a rented camera. If you still can't afford one, rent or borrow one, and get each of your parents on tape for your children to remember. Do it now before it's too late!

—————— Chapter 9 ——————

Making the Most of Your Children's

Toys

Removing Toy Madness

A child left to himself
brings shame to his mother . . .
—Prov. 29:15

Is one of the most annoying and ongoing messes in your home the multitude of toys that are all over your house? If your children or grandchildren own too many toys, here is a solution that I developed years ago that really works! When my older children were little, I tried several ideas that I had read in magazines, books, or heard on talk shows. **All of them** proved to be ideas that someone who had no children, or only one child, had thought up.

Now, years later, I still love learning more ways to organize and watching organization experts! Once again, some of their solutions are ridiculous and really are a joke.

Toy boxes are, to me, a joke. The children tend to play only with the top items, or they will pull out everything to get something on the bottom. For a few years, I tried the Montessori method and created shelves on our sun porch and *tried* to get them to put their toys back up on the shelf. Honestly, this was so much work that it was not really worth the effort—even though I had only two children and a lot more time to devote to toys.

A laundry basket, however, is great for a small child's toys (toddler) and contains just enough toys for him. Even the smallest children can learn to pick up their toys and put them in the basket, unless you don't make them do it when they pitch a fit. But just remember when you give in to them—if you can't manage an eighteen-month-old, how will you manage when they turn 18 *years* old?

Today, there is no doubt that children in the United States have way, way, way too many toys. I watch shows all the time when the parents say they need bigger rooms or a bigger house because of all the toys that their children have. How ridiculous! They get toys from parents who work, grandparents (who now have a limited amount of grandchildren that they have waited for, for years), and for their friends. Hand-me-downs, and yard sale toys can also create too many toys and way too much clutter.

So, again, the rooms are cluttered and there is no room to play because of all the plastic slides and other paraphernalia that parents wrongly believe are necessary for their children to have to keep them occupied and happy. Some of you may share my beliefs, but it is your parents or in-laws who are the culprits. There is an easy remedy if the grandparents live locally, and that is to tell them that whatever they buy needs to stay at *their* house. Oh what a joy it will be for your child to get to go to Grandma and Grandpa's house where there are so many toys! My ex-husband told me about going to his grandparent's house almost weekly. They had nothing to play with except a little footstool that he would flip over and play in as if it were a racing-car. Oh, how times have changed!!

I recently heard that baby showers for Grandma were becoming popular! Grandma gets toys and other baby furnishings for her house when the grandbabies come to visit. Yikes, this is scary.

Well, after twenty years of proven success, here is a sure way to control the toy problem in your home or in Grandma's home (if she wants help).

First. Sort all of your children's toys into categories or sets, or make a bunch of variety buckets. Use any kind of container you have, such as huge laundry soap buckets, Rubbermaid tubs, laundry buckets, and keep any sets in their original box if you have them (and if they fit back once assembled). Throw out any toys that are missing pieces or are broken beyond repair.

Now, lock'em up! Next, find a closet to put all the sorted toys into that with a lock, and bring out *one* set for an entire day. Horrified? You think they will not be happy until they can get their hands on every toy they want? A.D.D. (Attention Deficient Disorder) is not a disease but a behavior that we encourage and nurture in our children or grandchildren.

A child who is left to run from one event to another, to watch as much television as he wants, and has little or no discipline (even the word "no" is not used) is in for trouble or will soon be a student who needs to be "drugged" when they get to school and is incapable of sitting still for five minutes at a time.

The more you are blessed financially, the more your children will have, and the more destruction it will bring if you are not very, very careful. If your child is forced to play with one set, he or she is also forced to "be creative"! It usually comes over them quickly when they tell you that they are "bored." My cure for "boredom" is housework!

I immediately stop what I am doing, *enthusiastically* (with a big smile on my face) tell them "Great! I can use your help!" and get them going on a job. This method is not effective if you only "threaten" that they will work if they complain when bored. You must follow through for them to learn that complaining that they are bored is the natural consequence for not being creative and learning to entertain themselves.

If you are not as determined of a mother or grandmother as I am, you could easily modify this method and just let one set come out at a time. And unless it is all cleaned up, another one is not given out. But trust me, children who are forced to be creative (with only one set a day) are the most blessed.

Schedule. Now that your toys are organized and in sets, see how many sets you have, and assign each to a day for play. Here is an example of what we did:

Mondays: Legos
Tuesdays: Playhouse
Wednesdays: Space set
Thursdays: Cars (all Hot Wheels and trucks)
Fridays: Farm set
Saturdays: Airport

When my older four children were young, we would rotate on a one-week schedule. Now with my younger three, we have enough sets for a two-week rotation.

I also had a "music" day with all kinds of toys that made noise and another day for puzzles. I did not have these in the normal rotation but brought them out only periodically. I could rarely take the noisiness of the music day, but I loved the day they did puzzles all day long.

You may be thinking that you don't mind the toys, or you have enough room to let them have all their toys available every day. However, as I shared earlier, there are many more benefits when I followed the Lord's leading on this. It helped my children to learn contentment. So many children are "bored" even though they have a toy store in their own home. All they want is more, as they flitter from one activity to another. Love your children enough not to indulge their boredom; instead, stretch them through teaching contentment. It will also help the creativity that God put in them that is now lying dormant.

Missing pieces: No matter how hard you try, you will find pieces of sets under the couch or behind a table. Rather than trying to put it right back in the set, I put a bucket that I marked "Missing Pieces" and put it in the closet with the other toys. When the children or I found a piece that was missing, we put it into the bucket. Then each morning after I pulled out the set for the children, I would dump the bucket out on the floor so the children could look for pieces that belonged in the set they were playing with. Even Dad knew where to put something he found!

This kind of rotation can work with board games too, when your children get older. Just set a particular game for that day, and you will find that they get less bored with the same one.

This also helps when grandparents want to know what your children need for Christmas or birthdays. You can see what set needs more Legos or cars and get something that your children really need, instead of something that they won't play with.

Another great tip. Set aside a favorite or new set for when "Dad comes home." My husband told me once, when he worked outside the home, that sometimes he would dread walking through the front door at 5:30 p.m. because of the "mobbing" that would ensue. They would beg him to wrestle or play with them, which he would do because he loved them. However, he told me that if he just had a little time to unwind, he would be fine.

So the next night, I told the children that I was going to let them play with their favorite set "when Daddy came home." When they heard him come through the door, he was again mobbed with kisses and hugs, but then they ran away to Mommy who had just taken out their favorite set! They played happily until dinner was ready. Then, after dinner, they had a wonderful time with Daddy who had had time to relax after a hard day's work.

This also works when adult guests come to visit. Just take out a special set that is brought out for such occasions. Speaking of guests, when you have children visiting your home, you will LOVE this method with your toys being locked up.

When little friends come to play. Some children are extremely destructive and break toys, while some are literal tornadoes making a mess throughout your house. When friends come to play, make sure you insist that they help clean up the toys. Children who are made (maybe for the first time) to pick up toys will be less likely to destroy your home when they come back (if they come back).

You will probably have to supervise the clean-up, but you may be helping that mother who never thought her child was capable of picking up after himself. Make sure you teach your children to clean up when they are visiting. When other moms see how your children are trained, they may just ask for your help. Then you can send them to our site for free books, which we hope will lead to them coming to know the Man who died for them!

Where children play. Early on in my mothering, I made it a habit to have no toys in the child's bedroom, unless it was a doll or stuffed animal. I always kept the children's reading books in their room, and that was all. Bedrooms, my children learned, are for sleeping, resting, or reading. This saved their rooms from looking like most children's rooms—a disaster that I did not want to have to clean nor try to make them clean.

A great way to keep the stuffed animals and/or dolls off the floor and give them a home (while at the same time decorating their room) is to put small cup hooks around the door of their closet or window. Then tie a ribbon around their neck and hang them from the hook. I did this because we seemed to have fifty stuffed animals that would always end up on the floor. Rarely did my children ask me to take them down to play with, so when we moved, we donated them to the poor.

Even if you live in a very small apartment, you can carve out a place to play. If it is tiny, make it fun by laying out a large blanket or sheet on the floor and tell them they need to stay on it. Believe it or not, it makes things more fun. Another benefit is when it is time to clean up, especially if they have been playing with small pieces such as Legos—it's a snap to lift up and pour the pieces back in the container!

In closing, one very important task, even with toys, is to de-clutter your toys periodically. A good time is right before your children's birthday and again before Christmas. Then you can see what toys your child may benefit from having in your home, and rid your home of toys that are broken, missing pieces, no longer played with, or toys your child has outgrown. Give toys to the church or to charity since God blesses us for *giving,* not selling.

Use the method from Chapter 2 for sorting your toys, and especially focus on toys that your children have outgrown. Give such toys to friends, to the poor, or box them up for future children (but only if it will used within two years).

If your child is not playing with a toy, it is probably the biggest part of the mess you clean up, or step over every day. Do yourself and your children a favor by ridding yourself of toys they no longer use or need, then organizing and hiding the rest as suggested in this chapter.

Chapter 10

Making the Most of Your

Meal Planning—

Make it Simple

Thou dost prepare a table before me . . .
—Ps. 23:5

"Hey, what's for dinner?"

If you are like most women, **"What's for dinner?"** is a question that makes you cringe. Whether you are asking yourself, or your children or husband asks you, what's for dinner is a question that plagues every homemaker. Would you believe that over the course of your adult lifetime, you will make more than 18,000 dinners and almost 60,000 meals? That's a lot of ideas that you and I have to come up with!!

Knowing that there had to be a better way, I tried the method where you cook for a month, but cooking for an entire day—all day long—was horrible! If that weren't bad enough, when I tried it my family complained that they didn't want "leftovers" every night, since the meals were precooked and heated up!

My mother solved her "what's for dinner" dilemma by making the same few meals over and over again. Basically, we ate: spaghetti, hamburgers, pork chops, fish, and chicken. To have a particular meal set for a particular day would have been too organized for my mother, so she just mixed up the days, which was her way of keeping us guessing so we wouldn't know which day to find another family to feed us.

When I was in college I came to the conclusion that it was not "making" dinner that was tough, but instead it was "what" to make that was the root of the problem. I concluded that if I could just come up with enough dinner choices for one month, and repeat it each month, each dinner would be served only 12 times a year!

I also noticed when I watched old movies, like "Pollyanna," that the cook would have a clipboard that listed the meal, which the lady of the house would choose a week ahead. So, I set out to make a month's menu and put it on a clipboard to save time, money, and primarily the mental strain and anguish of knowing what to have for dinner—"viola"—it worked!

My method worked so well for me that I was asked to speak about my monthly menu to many women's organizations; however, I soon realized after my divorce that not all women enjoy organizing like I do and to just sit down and create this proven foolproof method. I also discovered that it is not always necessary to be that organized when you have the desire and freedom to come up with a variety of meals. Therefore, I knew I needed to seek the Lord for another method that would require less initial invested time, which would work for my family and yours!

Seek Him. Ladies, that is always the key and answer to every dilemma of your life—seek the Lord for the solution. Why ask yourself, your friend, or an expert when there is Someone just longing to bless you and give you secrets that no one else knows? If I have any wisdom at all it came from God. We love to bless each other with ideas and tips to make our lives easier, but the best one I could ever give you is to seek the Lord for every solution to every problem or question you have. Big or small, He has the answers and is sitting right beside you just waiting for you to ask!

Level 1
EASIEST Meal Planning Ever
10 Easy Steps

Goal: to find least 28 dinner ideas, which will include out-to-eat days.

1. Take a 3x5 card and write on the top a **theme** for your meal: chicken, ground beef, Mexican, Italian, pasta, meatless, on the grill, casseroles, nice meals, crock-pot, family favorites, comfort food (what you ate growing up), and another for eating out.

2. On each 3x5 card brainstorm and write down all the meals you can think of that are either chicken, ground beef, Mexican, Italian, pasta, meatless, on the grill, casseroles, nice meals, crock-pot, family favorites, comfort food (what you ate growing up), and places your family likes to go when eating out.

For dinner ideas: check any list you might have made, think of what you usually make, ask your family or friends for ideas, look in cookbooks, and think of places you eat out and what you order to trigger your memory. Everyone who does this simple exercise is surprised by how many dinners they actually have listed!

Now, look at your cards to see which theme has the most dinner ideas listed. For your once-a-month-menu you'll need just 7 themes, one for each day of the week, which would include your eating out card if you'd like to eat out once a week.

By the way, you may notice that some of your meals overlap. For instance, you may have fried chicken on your chicken card and on your nice meal card. Not to worry, we cover this on a later step.

More about eating out. If your family, right now, goes out to eat *all the time,* plan at least 2 out-to-eat days per week. If you're the kind who *never* eats out, you might want to think about taking a break from cooking and also forgo the negative comments grown children love to bring up making you feel guilty about.

Eating leftovers. Include a day to eat your leftovers by creating a food bar, which is what I did (for our Friday lunch) for years until just recently. If you don't want to eat your leftovers, find someone to give them to. For almost ten years I gave all my leftovers to my parents so my mom would not have to cook. The truth was that I always made extra, and included my leftovers that fed my mom, dad, and my retarded sister!

Since my parents are now deceased, I began giving my leftovers to my oldest son who works from home and is too busy to cook. He said it saves him so much time and money by just grabbing a meal and heating it up.

A friend of mine never made lunches. Leftovers were always their lunches. Once again, don't try to figure it out. Ask God to tell you what to do with your leftovers!

3. Choose your theme according to the day of the week. For instance, you might want the crock-pot recipes on Wednesday because that night is crazy when you go to church mid-week, or maybe you would choose the crock-pot meal for Sunday afternoon when you get home from church. Or, you might want it on Monday night so you can make it ahead of time on Sunday night since Mondays are always exhausting. Get the picture? Here is how I have mine:

Sunday is our only **out-to-eat** after church.
Monday we have **Italian** because it's quick and easy.
Tuesday is **chicken** for no special reason—we just like and eat chicken a lot.
Wednesday we have **Mexican**, which is also an easy meal.
Thursday seems to be the only night all of my children are home, so that is our **nice meal**.
Friday is **family favorites,** which is our way of celebrating the end of the work/school week.
Saturday I like to **grill** (and yes, I do it in the dead of winter).

Another leftover tip: Your leftover day should be the day before (or day of) grocery shopping so that you have cleaned out your old food, wiped down the shelves, all before putting in the fresh food (instead of what most people do—burying food that spoils).

Remember to also clean out your breadbasket, chip shelf, fruit drawer, salad/vegetable drawer, and meat/cheese drawer that can also be used for leftovers or given to someone in need.

Write on the *top left*, what day of the week you choose for each theme.

4. Next, make a separate card for each meal. If you have at least four meals for each theme, it will cover a month of menus. If you have 6 meals, it will stretch for a month and a half. Depending on how many meal choices you have, you can stretch it as far as you have meals for! This also includes the places your family eats out.

5. Take your theme meals and paperclip them together. Place these in a plastic 3x5 card file under the section "dinners." Then, just once a week (we do this on Saturdays after our big breakfast), pull one of the meals from your theme for each day of the week. For instance:

Sunday: I'd choose "Chinese Chef" from my **out-to-eat** cards.
Monday: I'd choose "lasagna" from my **Italian** cards.
Tuesday: I'd choose "fried chicken" from my **chicken** cards.
Wednesday: I'd choose "beef tacos" from my **Mexican** cards.
Thursday: I'd choose "pork roast" from my **nice meal** cards.
Friday: I'd choose "tuna fish cakes" from my **family favorites** cards.
Saturday: I'd choose "steaks" from my **grill** cards.

6. Complete meals. If you want less to think about each day, then under the meal write *what you'll have* with each dinner. First find the vegetables by brainstorming and writing down every vegetable that you can think of on a 3x5 card. Don't limit you're family by what they currently eat; begin to try something new and expand your family's horizon.

Follow the vegetables with a starch: pasta, rice, bread, or potato, and finally, if you'd like, a dessert. Write this at the bottom of your card. For instance, I list hot tea, fortune cookies, and chopsticks with a Chinese meal. Use your 3x5 card to help you by making notes (in pencil) to yourself to save time thinking of these things each week. For instance:

Sunday: is simply Chinese Chef.
Monday: next to the lasagna I would write salad, and bread.
Tuesday: next to fried chicken I'd write spinach, and corn bread.
Wednesday: next to beef tacos I'd write refried beans, tortilla chips with salsa and guacamole.
Thursday: next to pork roast I'd write pasta side dish, salad, and rolls.
Friday: next to tuna fish cakes I'd write elbow macaroni with tomato sauce.
Saturday: next to steaks I'd write baked potatoes, salad, and rolls.

7. **Lunch.** Another *simple* idea to make the most of our time is to brainstorm for your lunch meals in the same way as you did for your dinners. To find **lunch ideas**, begin by asking each of your children their favorites, but make sure they are alone when you ask them. Since we have home schooled since 1989, and have worked at home for almost as long, I have always tried to have ONE of each of my children's "favorites" once a week. (However, they are strictly warned not to complain when they eat something they don't particularly like on someone else's day).

If you can't come up with a month's worth of different lunches to correspond with your dinners, just repeat the lunches that everyone seems to like the most. Make a card for each lunch and then match with the dinner with that lunch. A big meat dinner should be combined with a pasta or meatless lunch. Again, a light lunches go with a heavy dinners OR big lunch with lighter dinner. For instance:

Sunday lunch: is our out-to-eat. So, for dinner we always have Sunday snacks (those frozen meals that the kids love but I hate. So I just eat some leftovers or a salad.
Monday lunch: is a fast food lunch since my daughters and I do our grocery shopping.
Tuesday lunch: is hot dog day: hot dogs, corn dogs, chilidogs, or specialty dogs.
Wednesday lunch: is a meat sandwich: ham, chicken, chicken salad, tuna, roast beef or turkey.

Thursday lunch: is a boxed meal.

Friday lunch: has always been our leftover day, but when my children got so sick of it, I prayed and the Lord led me to give our family's leftovers to my grown son who just heats them up in the microwave. Now we have PBJ (peanut butter and jelly) or the leftover meat for sandwiches.

Saturday lunch: we don't have lunch. We eat our big breakfast very late and have an early dinner.

8. **Breakfast.** Now make the most of your precious time and do the last bit of brainstorming for breakfast ideas. To make it easier, I began creating a **breakfast** theme. For instance:

Sunday breakfast: is each person's choice since everyone is ready for church at different times.

Monday breakfast: is just cereal (not sugar cereal; see Friday).

Tuesday breakfast: is a boxed muffin or quick bread mix that my 13-year-old son makes.

Wednesday breakfast: is toast since we make our homemade bread on Tuesdays for sandwiches.

Thursday breakfast: is hot cereal or fruit and yogurt in the summer.

Friday breakfast: has been sugar cereal day for over twenty years.

Saturday breakfast: is our BIG family breakfast. We basically rotate between homemade buttermilk biscuits, scones, pancakes, and French toast (our recipes are in an upcoming chapter).

Here's another example from when we lived on our farm:

Sundays: Donuts, it's the Lord's Day so REJOICE and make it special!

Mondays: Toast (keep it interesting by trying different kinds of bread like raisin or sour dough).

Tuesdays: Cereal (if you don't have cereal everyday, then only open just one box at a time, or at the most two).

Wednesdays: Baked goods (This is when we have something baked from a box mix. Have one of your young girls learn to bake by having her make this for the family. When everyone praises her, she will begin to want to learn to bake more and learn to cook! This works for sons too!)

Thursdays: Hot cereal or frozen waffles.

Fridays: Sugar Cereal

Saturdays: Big breakfast (This is when I make a big hot breakfast like my buttermilk biscuits, scones, pancakes, and French toast, along with bacon or ham, juice—the works!)

*Cereal Tip: I just found a great cereal tip—again through prayer. I now remove the bag from the box, which makes more room in the pantry, helps to see when there are really only crumbs left, and helps remind children to keep the bag closed tightly.

I rip off the box top (that has the name on it), then clip it to the bag, which requires two clothespins thus keeping the bag closed and the cereal fresher!

If possible, try to only make a "once-a-week big breakfast." If you are married, make sure your husband is agreeable. Some men do physical labor and need a hardy breakfast, like my neighbor's husband when we lived on our farm. Remember to adjust all my "recommendations" with your family and what works for you. If you do pick one day a week for your big breakfast, try not to pick Sundays when you go to church!

9. With all your meals planned, the rest is so easy! Just thumb through your dinner cards, lunch cards, and breakfast cards choosing a meal for each day.

10. The final step so you don't need to answer the "What's for dinner" question would be to write your ***next day's*** **meals** on a small dry/erase board when you finish cleaning up each night after dinner.

Save more time and stress and pull your ingredients out onto the counter, and thaw any meat. This simple board keeps me a step ahead of any stress and eliminates my family asking what's for dinner (or any other meal).

By investing just a bit more of your time, you can make the most of your time by making a monthly meal plan that you can use over and over and over again. Why not go to step two?

Level 2
Monthly Meal Planning

If you'd like to invest just a little bit more time, you will be able to eliminate the weekly decisions and plan your menu for a month or even more depending on how many meal ideas you have. This is what I did for most of my married life, which made the most of my life and my precious time! Rather than pulling the cards each week, create a month's menu.

1. On your kitchen table or counter, take all your dinner cards and arrange them on your table like a calendar (Sunday – Saturday) for as many weeks as you have. Remember to look at the meals to see what fits your schedule (sport or church night easier meals; days most family members are home for the nicer big meals).

2. Once they are laid out, rearrange the meals to keep it varied and interesting. You would be surprised how this little extra planning ahead will bring about so many benefits for you and for your family!

Also, be sure to include those out-to-eat days. To determine how often: if your family, right now, goes out *all of the time* plan at least two out-to-eat days per week. If you **never** eat out, as I said earlier, do it at least once a month or your children will certainly bring that up negatively when they are grown.

If you have young children, choose your out to eat day on a day when children eat free or at a discount. Special offers are everywhere if you just look (more on this below).

3. Move the meals with fresh vegetables closer to your shopping day, followed by the frozen/canned vegetables that you can use later. I keep vegetables that are fresh (like yellow squash and zucchini, an artichoke or whole cauliflower) within two days of my shopping day (when arranging my meal order) with the frozen vegetables later.

4. Once your cards are done and are laid out, then type up a permanent list. You can also post the list on your refrigerator that will answer that all time favorite question *"What's for Dinner?"* rather than using the dry/erase board, which can save you even more time.

5. To make this system flexible, simply cross off all the meals that you end up making and place a BOX around each meal that you have to skip. Many of us have things that come up so we may have to miss a meal that we have planned. Your schedule should work for you and not be another burden in your life. The beauty of a skipped meal is that you can pick all of them up at the end of the week or at the end of the month making your list of meals last even longer.

My four-week menu (that I used for more than five years) usually lasted about five weeks since very often we would have to skip that dinner for a variety of reasons.

Just be sure that if your skipped meal included fresh meat, put the meat in the freezer or do the fresh meat meal the next day and skip (box) the next day's meal.

Level 3
List the Ingredients
Who will prepare?
How much of each?

1. To simplify your life, sit down for another 30 minutes and list all the ingredients on the back of each card. I turn my length wise. That works well. If you want a simpler method, write the list of ingredients down on the day you make each meal for the first time, then add to it things you may have forgotten the first time around. This easy step will help you immensely when preparing your shopping list, making sure you don't forget anything.

2. If your husband likes to cook or you have an older or adult child who can prepare any of the meals, write who will be preparing the meal in the *upper left* hand corner of your 3x5 card and be sure to post their name on your calendar or Meal Sheet next to the date.

Also, to help prepare your younger children for adulthood, list the name of the child who could *help you* prepare each meal also in the *upper left* hand corner under your name.

*When choosing a child for any chore in your home, **always** start with the youngest child or least mature to see if they could manage it. Parents always overuse their oldest child (or children) not only overburdening them, but also creating spoiled, unappreciative and immature younger children.*

3. To help with **quantity**, each time you prepare a meal write down (in PENCIL) how much you used to prepare the meal to help you the next time you make it. If you end up short, then erase and increase the amount. If you end up with quite a bit of leftovers, then decrease the portions.

Using your cards to write out any important information, like how many chicken breasts to cook or how many eggs you scrambled, helps so much if efficiency and cutting down even more the mental stress of homemaking. As your family grows and your needs change, you can easily adjust your cards. For instance:

For fried chicken use a half of a chicken breast per child, one per adult.
For hamburgers use a half a pound of Ground *Round* per person and one bun each.
For ravioli, count 4 for each adult, 3 per child or a small eater.

To avoid fat or overweight children (and adults) do not serve "family style" by putting everything out on the table. Instead, I have always put the plates out in a row on the counter and put a portion on each plate. This also insures that everyone is getting vegetables!

I leave any extra on the stove so that if anyone is getting seconds (yourself included) the person is easily noticed while getting more. In addition, my children were never allowed to just go and get food from the cupboard or refrigerator. They were taught to ask first which helped me monitor not only overeating, but also eating too close to dinner.

Sugar

Since my husband and I came from totally different backgrounds, I was unprepared for sugar cereal that my children wanted every morning like Daddy used to have. I am not sure how we came to this and how he ended up agreeing to it (it had to be GOD!), but years ago, we made Fridays mornings "sugar cereal day!"

It is often better to not make some things taboo unless you and your husband are in complete agreement—if you are, thank the Lord, because most couples are not! Instead, make it a "treat" or "reward." God loves to bless us, so this may be an area where you can bless your children!

Our children don't feel deprived, nor are they "weird," but are learning to live with self-control and moderation rather than excess, which is the way the world lives. To forbid is to become religious, which is how rebellion starts.

Make "sugar cereal day" a special day like a Monday, so they pop out of bed, or a Friday, because they made it through the week! This goes for colas or sodas or pop (whatever you call it). Rather than eliminate it, have it for special occasions.

Teaching moderation and control, I believe, is better than forbidding something completely. My children were allowed coke with their pizza once a week. Now that we know sodas causes stomach cancer (not just cavities or obesity in children), we chose to basically cut it out completely and replaced it with sweetened tea once a week. The rest of the time they drink lots of water!

Taking a Break: Go Out to Eat

As I mentioned earlier in this chapter, it is always good to take a break from cooking, and actually schedule a day, or even two, to go out to eat each week.

Most families are out of balance and either eat out ALL THE TIME, or never eat out. Of course, sometimes it is because your husband loves your home cooked meals.

If you go out too often, it is often because you are not prepared. The method that I have shared with you should help, but as I said earlier, don't try to stop going out to eat completely; instead, set specific out to eat days and take a much deserved break.

Sometimes, we women need to go out to eat; but very often, where you go and how you order will determine how often you feel you can go out. Because of our large family, we always tend to gravitate to the 99¢ menus that are in most fast food restaurants, and we ALWAYS **order water**. We used to do so due to the sheer cost of 9 beverages, now it is due to health issues. Not only is it proven to cause stomach cancer, that amount of sugar also cuts the immune system down by 50%. If my children were to drink a soda now and then, I would prefer that they are at home so they don't pick up outside diseases and an entire liter cost what one drink would in a restaurant.

Also, when they were all young I always gave them a couple of choices of what they could order. We also go where kids eat free, especially when we had so many under 10 or 12.

There are many national fast food chains and local restaurants that want to entice families, so they offer free or inexpensive kid's meals. I see them all the time on signs. Call the restaurants in your area to see if they have a Kid's Night. Be sure to find out what day, the time it starts, the ages (be extremely clear on this point), and whether the drink is included or not. I've ordered water for my children when they could have had a soft drink (a real treat).

The wisest solution is to find all this *over the phone* so you don't look cheap or end up eating at a restaurant on the wrong night—it's happened to me! Then write all the details out on your 3x5 card for each restaurant. With a pencil, write out what the children like to order! This helps when you take them out and especially if Grandma or Dad wants to take your little ones out to eat

Chapter 11

Making the Most of

Grocery Shopping

Creating a Customized List

Most people make a new list each time they run to the store, or they may use a standard printed list that comes in an organizer which makes a bit more sense. With just a little bit of invested time, you can create a master grocery list eliminating the need to brainstorm each week. Even using a standard list requires mental energy to fill in the blanks of what your family needs, which usually results in items forgotten leading to a quick run to the store just before dinner!

In addition, lists that you make or the standard variety do not list the aisles where these items are located. With a customized list, we weave through the store saving half the time normally spent, and eliminating having to retrace your steps when you missed something on a particular aisle. There is an easier way!

1. Create a master grocery list by walking through your grocery store, just once, with a clipboard. Walk up and down the aisles writing down the items that you purchase on each side of the aisle. Note the number of the aisle.

*Make your list when you are not at the store to buy your groceries!

2. Go home and type your list on computer (or write it out by hand) and make copies. Don't print a whole year's worth since (each time you shop) you will see things you missed or want to change on your list. Make about a month's worth and clip it on a clipboard to hang somewhere convenient: by your desk, in your kitchen or maybe in your laundry room.

This half an hour of invested will save you dozens of hours of shopping, and hours of brainstorming each time you run to the store!

3. Use this list each week by reading through the week's ingredients that you have listed on the back of your 3x5 meal cards and ***highlight*** your list with things that you need. To make sure you don't run out of anything, go down your printed list and ***cross out*** what you don't need that week and highlight everything else that you see you need.

4. After shopping, save each week's list in the back of the clipboard and use these to periodically update your list with things you no longer use and add those things that you may have started buying. *I had diapers on my list for almost a year after I no longer had a baby in diapers!*

5. Rather than running to the store, or running out of things, ***choose*** one day each week to do your grocery shopping. Try to pick a day when you are not too rushed (never plan anything you don't have to do on a Monday). Weekends or after 5 are the busiest days at the grocery store, so if you can avoid these days and times it will make shopping much easier.

If you love a bargain, hit the grocery store early in the morning (while your family is still sleeping). In most stores, around 6–7 a.m., you can head straight to the meat counter and get meats at a ***reduced*** price. I buy the more expensive ground beef, like sirloin, for less than the cheapest ground beef. (If you're not a morning person, hit the store early just once a month and stock up on your meat.) Another added benefit of shopping early is that it is always less crowded. If you can't go that early, late morning is also good. Just try to *never* grocery shop on the weekends or after 5 p.m. on weekdays.

Tips for the Holidays

Take advantage of holidays like Halloween, Christmas, Valentine's Day and Easter—and "divide the spoil!" ". . . And she who remains at home will divide the spoil"! (Ps. 68:12).

The day after every holiday, the first thing the morning, we go to the grocery store and buy candy or decorations for 50–75% off! Chocolate candy last for months in the freezer and normally lasts from one holiday to the next. This is especially perfect since very often the more expensive candies are left, but are less expensive than the cheap candy if you bought it just a day earlier!

I also buy all my wrapping paper, ribbon, bows, and tags the day after Christmas and store it in my Christmas boxes for the next year. Also, I try to find wrapping paper, gift bags, or other decorations (like paper plates) that don't look like a particular holiday and use them for birthdays.

In October, many of the fast food chains offer coupon books for just a dollar for trick-or-treaters. For many years we lived in the middle of nowhere, and before that we had a German Shepherd in our yard, which meant we had no trick-or-treaters! One year, I bought a dollar booklet for 12 orders of fries, and we used them afterwards. Now, it is a tradition. Some burger chains offer fries; others offer an ice cream cone, cookies, or fries.

Watch the expiration date. Some last until the end of November; others will go to the end of the year.

With bags of fries for less than a dime, along with 99¢ burgers, you can't make it that cheap at home! This can come in handy with all the hustle and bustle of the holidays. Isn't God good?

Tips on Lists

The method above is the way I keep my home stocked with food and toiletry items my family needs; however, I also use a dry/erase marker board as a way for my family to communicate that we are out of something.

Place your board on the side of your refrigerator or in your laundry room). As you, your husband, or children notice something that you are running out of or need—just write it on your marker board. Our older children are great about calling home and asking what is on the board to see if they can pick it up for me ahead of my regular shopping day.

Tips on Where to Shop

If you like to save money, choose a store where you bag it yourself. Not only do I like to save money, I also like to organize my bags according to where it goes in my kitchen to save steps when I get home.

If you have several places to shop, like going to a discount bread store, go to these first if at all possible. Even Sam's Club may not have what I have on my list, so going there first will enable me to transfer what I need onto my grocery store list.

Tips for Your Weekly Shopping Day

Making my list and shopping in one day took too much of my time, more effort, and I often felt rushed. So a few years ago I divided the task into *two* days. It made all the difference in the world! I take more time and effort to make sure that I have everything on my list. I also found that I rarely missed items that I needed.

With a new printed list, go to your marker board and transfer the items written down onto your list with a highlighter, and then erase them.

Next, use your printed list checking your pantry and refrigerator against the "needed ingredients" for that week's menu.

If you use coupons, put a "C" next to the item and then clip your coupons on your clipboard. This helps to make sure you are choosing the correct item that it is being offered, and to make sure you hand your coupons to the cashier.

For the hot summer months, I invested in coolers and cooler bags to get my frozen foods and refrigerated foods home safely.

It also helps to have a couple of rectangle laundry baskets in your trunk to put your plastic bags into, which will save you time and effort getting the bags into the house. It also prevents the items from spilling out while driving home.

Including your Children

If you'd like to use this as a "learning experience" for your child, give your child the clipboard, along with a pencil, and the coupons while you push the cart. Have your child tell you the next item you'll be looking for and the coupon brand or requirement (buy two get one free).

If you have other children, let them be the one to get the item and put it into the cart. Have your helpers hand the coupons to the cashier, and be sure that your children unload your shopping cart.

When unloading the car on shopping day, my family has been taught to help. They place all the bags on the counters or table, and once the car is empty, they take all the food out of the bags. The older children (or I) place the food in the cupboards in an orderly fashion. I have a labeled shelf for cereal, for chips, for canned goods, for baking, etc.

If you have several children that can help, break down this job for efficiency and speed. I had my tallest put away cokes and chips that went in the cupboard over our refrigerator. My organized daughter put canned goods away, always being very careful to have them sorted properly with the labels facing forward. Another child put away all refrigerated items, and the guy who's always in a hurry put away the freezer stuff. The youngest child collects all the discarded plastic bags.

Prepare Ahead

If you cook your ground beef when you get home from the market, it will not only be ready to throw together in a meal, but it also tastes fresher, and it can be kept longer in the refrigerator without spoiling. (At one time I paid one of my sons to do this. He needed the money, and I particularly hated this job.)

Cooked ground beef also keeps well in the freezer; use zip lock bags to save space and eliminate buying a lot of plastic containers. Just recently we had a party where we served tacos. I made extra on purpose to be sure I didn't run out, and also because I knew I could use the meat later. Since I cooked the meat up fresh, I was able to bag up the leftover seasoned meat and have three dinner's worth still in my freezer—I love it!

Make up your meatloaf, pour the sauce over you bar-b-q ribs, make up your lasagna, and put them in the refrigerator. This not only makes it easier on cooking day; it enhances the flavor of your meal.

Joy!

The most important thing you can do is to *enjoy* the job God has given you, and find "joy" in it! By being incredibly prepared and staying ahead of this all-important task of purchasing the food and preparing meals for your family, you will be less likely to hate the job. Anything that you are good at, you'll enjoy doing. On the flip side, things that you struggle with in your life, you can' help but hate.

Once you use this chapter to master this task, begin to enjoy the challenge of preparing fun things in fun ways. Cut your sandwiches into special shapes with a cookie cutter. If your children hate the crust, cut out different shapes in the middle, then take the crust and roll them into a "wrap" that they will eat!

In the summer, purchase plastic burger baskets for lunches or for a burger dinner for fun. Put a sucker in the basket for a fun dessert.

As I mentioned in the last chapter, keep your children from overeating and save on "serving dishes," rather than placing the food on the table "Country Style," line your plates up on the counter in order of age, and serve each child the appropriate portions. Even husbands will eat less and keep their weight down with this method. And if anyone does want "seconds," they have to make the effort (and call attention) to it by going back to the kitchen or stove.

With your meals and shopping organized, you can now find enjoyment by creating delicious, nutritious, gourmet, and fun meals.

Finally, be sure to set your table early in the day and make it pretty, fun, and inviting for your family. That will show them just how much you really care!

——— Chapter 12 ———

Making the Most of

Your Oven

Delicious Breakfast Treats

There is nothing that you can learn or teach your daughters to do that will bring you more praise and satisfaction than learning to bake from scratch. I have to laugh at how every home needs to have this state of the art kitchen with stainless steal appliances, yet most girls today have no idea how to cook or bake! Crazy!

Since I, too, was one of these crazy girls who didn't know how to cook and never baked one thing in my life before I married (which included even a box mix), I learned how easy it really was and how terribly satisfying it is. That is why I taught my daughters to bake at a young age, which led to them wanting to cook.

When you think about it, an education is not as important as learning and mastering something that you are going to do everyday, up to three times a day. Store bought (as my late Great-Grandma Brown used to call it) tastes absolutely nothing like baked from scratch. The prepared or box mixes are not that much better; however, for some baked treats they do turn out better than scratch: cakes and piecrust to be specific.

The pie recipe in this chapter was my first success at baking, which gave me the courage to try more things. The Lord was with me (and giving me the desires of my heart) one date night, when I was still married, and my husband stumbled on a blue ribbon recipe book in large bookstore. It was full of baked goods that had won a blue ribbon at the state fair. I changed them just a bit by making everything just a bit sweeter!

The rest of the recipes I am sharing are those that women have given me over the years as I confessed to not being able to bake. Ladies, I am now known for my delicious baked goods. Therefore, any one of you, just by following the recipe, can bless your family and friends. "Her children rise up and bless her; her Husband also, and he praises her, saying: 'Many daughters have done nobly, but you excel them all'" (Prov. 31:28–29).

Erin's Buttermilk Pancakes (and Waffles)

Every time I make these pancakes, I get rave reviews. The same lady who helped me bake my first pie gave this recipe to me, but it was as a whole-wheat pancake. This makes quite a bit to feed a family or to use as a quick breakfast during your busy week. They can be reheated in the microwave, but are tastier when put them in the toaster lightly done!

2 C flour
2 C buttermilk
2 eggs
2 T. oil
1 t. baking soda
1 t. baking powder
1 t. salt
1 t. vanilla

It's so easy. Put all the ingredients in a mixing bowl with the mixer on slow, then on high. Once it is completely mixed, do not mix again. Cook on a 350° griddle. This batter can be poured on a waffle iron for light and crispy waffles (if you want them more chewy increase the oil). I usually make up extra batter, and use the leftover to make up waffles to keep in the freezer to just pop in the toaster.

Ever since we moved to Missouri, I have had to add more liquid for the consistency that my family likes. If you like them "cakey," use less liquid. If you like them thin, use more liquid.
I also found that I had lighter pancakes when I use self-rising flour for 1/4 of the flour. Use unbleached white flour for a more natural,

flavorful taste, or go organic for the same great flavor, which is now what I use.

Pancake Variations: To make Swedish pancakes: remove one fourth of the flour and add an extra egg; they are thinner and taste a bit more "eggy."

For a real treat, I make the second half of the batch chocolate chips pancakes! My children rave about them to all of their friends!! I like using the "mini" chocolate chips! When you have made all the plain pancakes that you want, then pour some chocolate chips into your batter and fold them in. These are my favorites too!!

For waffles: I had heard that it would require more oil, so I experimented with it. With my new Belgium waffle maker, the best consistency, I believe, is when the oil ratio stays the same. They are a bit crispy on the outside but tender on the inside. However, with my old regular waffle iron, they were *too* crispy. Test this yourself; keep all the other ingredients the same, just vary one tablespoon of oil and increase it according to your family's taste!

Melt-in-Your-Mouth Buttermilk Biscuits

You can't live in the South without knowing how to make good biscuits. I used to love biscuits, and I ordered them whenever we went out. Then, I learned to make my own! Now I don't enjoy eating anyone else's. These will give you rave reviews.

One night, we were asked to bring something for a homeschool potluck. I made up a huge batch of these biscuits. A lady came over to our table to ask why my children had snuck up to the buffet line and were hiding something under their napkins. They each had smuggled two biscuits before anyone could get them! Needless to say, she (and most of the mothers there) begged me for the recipe!

On another occasion, my second son, Axel, used to help pick up day-old baked goods from a local bakery to give to the poor. An older man would pick him up quite early for the task. One morning, I got up early and made up a batch of these biscuits and some delicious coffee (I'll give you the secret to great coffee after the scones below) to share with his elderly driver. The following week, my son panicked when he noticed this gentleman sitting out front almost an hour before they were scheduled to go—it was still dark! He was waiting for the biscuits, and this time he brought his own mug for my coffee!

2 C flour
1 T. baking powder
1/4 t. baking soda
3/4 t. salt
1 T. sugar
1/3 C shortening
1 C buttermilk

Preheat oven to 450°. Sift flour, powder, soda, salt, and sugar. Using a hand-held pastry blender, cut in shortening until mixture resembles coarse crumbs. Make a well (or hole) in the dry ingredients to hold the liquid, and pour in the buttermilk. Using a fork, stir quickly until the dough follows the fork around the bowl. (If you make huge batches like I do, then use a large serving fork to make it so much easier to mix!)

Turn the batter onto a lightly floured surface. Knead **gently** 10–12 times. (If you over knead quick breads they may look great, but they are like rubber. So do NOT over knead biscuits, scones, or the damper—any quick bread.) Pat the dough about 1/2 inch thick (you can use a rolling pin to make them an even thickness).

Dip a round biscuit cutter (or use the top of a glass like my mother did) into the flour between every few cuts. Cut dough straight down; do not twist the cutter.

Place one inch apart on an ungreased baking sheet. Bake in preheated oven 12–15 minutes at 450° or until they are light golden brown on top. (If they are ever doughy inside, it may be that they are too thick, so just pat or roll them thinner the next time.)

Scottish Scones

I found this recipe in a magazine many years ago. My family fell in love with it. One night, I met a woman from Scotland, and she begged me for the recipe. It seems her husband, an American, was disappointed that she was unable to make him Scottish Scones. A few weeks later, when I walked into the store where she worked, I thought she was going to leap over the counter when she saw me. She said that this recipe totally changed their marriage, and she is now married to "the happiest man on earth!" However, a few months later, she said that he had put on quite a few pounds!

2 C flour
2 t. baking powder
1/4 t. baking soda
1/2 t. salt
2 T. sugar

_____

1/3 C butter (6 T. sliced thin)
3/4 C buttermilk
1 large egg, lightly beaten
A little milk for the top

Combine the top five ingredients; then, cut in the butter with a pastry cutter until very fine. Add the buttermilk and egg. Stir with a fork until moist. Knead only **five** to **six** times (no more). Divide the dough in half; pat each half into a circle. Cut each circle into eight (pizza type) wedges with a sharp knife that you continue to dip in flour. Place them an inch apart on a lightly greased cookie sheet. Brush with milk and sprinkle sugar over the top. Bake at 425° for 12–15 minutes. Serve hot!

*If you had my recipe from a previous edition you may notice that I didn't say anything about having the butter VERY cold, which I heard made all the difference in the world regarding texture. This made the cutting in VERY hard so I really didn't like making these. Then one day while praying about a way to cut them in easier, the Lord had me try softening the butter. Ladies, neither my family nor I could taste or see any difference! They now are as easy as the buttermilk biscuits to make! Isn't God awesome when we seek Him for the answers to our dilemmas?!

Overnight Coffee Cake

Every Easter, instead of celebrating with eggs and the bunny, we have a Hallelujah Breakfast—Jesus has risen! I make this up the night before. It is simply delicious!

We also have a turkey for a Thanksgiving dinner. We thank the Lord for dying on the cross, and thank God for sending His Son. We are too busy to do it on Easter Sunday this year, so we will celebrate our Hallelujah Breakfast on Saturday.

2 C flour
1 C sugar
1/2 C firmly packed brown sugar
1 t. baking soda
1 t. baking powder
1/2 t. salt

---

1 C buttermilk
1/2 C butter (1 stick & 2 T)
2 large eggs

1/2 C firmly packed brown sugar
1 t. cinnamon

Combine the first six ingredients; next, add buttermilk, butter, and eggs. Beat at low speed with an electric mixer until moist; beat at medium speed another three minutes. Spoon or pour the batter into a greased and floured 13x9x2 pan. Combine the last two ingredients, and spread it over the batter with your hand. Cover and refrigerate overnight. Uncover and bake at 350° for 30–35 minutes or until a wooden pick comes out clean from the center. Serve warm.

Australian Damper

This is basically a large biscuit recipe from "down under." Ladies, it's so EASY—there are only three ingredients!

Cut two sticks of butter or margarine into six cups of self-rising flour
with a pastry blender until crumbly. Add one cup of buttermilk and
stir with a fork until moist. Knead three–four times (no more). Cut
dough in half and form two round mounds. Cut an "x" in the top of
both with a steak knife. Brush with milk, then sprinkle with sugar.
Bake at 425° for 25–28 minutes until slightly brown. Serve warm with
jam.

Tip: When cleaning up flour from the surface after you are done
kneading, use a DRY cloth or paper towel for easy clean up. Move the
trashcan next to the counter and wipe. Then follow up with a wet
cloth afterwards.

Tip: When washing anything that is greasy, wipe it as clean as you
can with a paper towel (or the cheaper napkin). Grease is what clogs
drains, and if you have a septic, what prevents food from being
absorbed into the earth.

French Toast

I buy the long French loaves that are already partially cut on a
diagonal, but any kind of bread will do.

Mix three eggs
3/4 cup milk (make it sometimes with buttermilk for a different
flavor)
1 1/2 teaspoon vanilla

Dip and cook on a 350° "buttered" griddle. I rip half of the butter
wrapper off and rub it over the hot griddle. It makes it tasty!

By using different breads, you can make many different kinds of
French toast. My favorite is using cinnamon raisin bread, and my
family likes Texas toast (that is just white bread cut thicker) and even
simple white bread!

Sprinkle powdered sugar for a beautiful presentation or cinnamon
sugar on the top for a different taste.

Great Coffee

It is important when you want to be a good hostess to be able to make great coffee—whether you drink it or not. Great-Grandma Brown tried to hint that I needed help with my coffee during one of her yearly visits before she passed away. Once I got the hint, I said, "Grandma, please tell me what to do!" This is what she told me.

First, make sure your coffee pot stays clean. If used daily, clean it once a month by pouring vinegar through followed by two water brews.

Next, make sure the strength is not too strong, not too weak, but "just right." Measure one rounded kitchen teaspoon per cup of coffee. We recently bought a coffee scoop that equals 3 rounded teaspoons full of coffee.

*However, since coffee has become so popular with espresso and the darker richer coffees being more popular, I began DOUBLING this recipe.

Now, for the final secret—this was the Lord's doing. We used to have cell group meetings in our home way back when we lived in California. Our group consisted of two coffee addicts! I was totally unprepared for our first meeting. I could quickly see that I was going to run out of regular coffee. After I prayed, I thought I might "stretch" the regular coffee by mixing half regular and half decaffeinated together. Everyone went WILD! The group drank all the coffee I had in the house that night!

I began to buy one can of each (decaffeinated and regular) and mix them together, until I realized that the coffee companies make 1/2 and 1/2 now (half caff). If you are buying your coffee and mixing, just make sure you buy two different brands when selecting your decaffeinated and regular. I store my coffee in the freezer to keep it fresh after opening.

Ever since that night, I have given this secret of great coffee out to my friends. Those who follow the above steps come back to tell me the praises they now receive for their coffee!

Tip: Grandma Brown also made me buy new dish towels. I used the thick ones (terry cloth) that were intended for drying hands, not dishes. Dish towels are very thin, and they don't leave lint. I bought a bundle of them at a warehouse store years ago, and they lasted for years!

Chapter 13

Making the Most of

Your Oven Part 2

Impressive & Luscious Desserts

Delicious Deep Dish Apple Pie

As I shared with you earlier, this was my first attempt at baking with the help of a friend. So I am placing it at the beginning of the chapter so that you, too, will gain the courage and confidence to begin baking from scratch.

1 pkg. Pillsbury pie crust (these are not the crusts already in a pie pan. They are folded in plastic wrap. You can find them in the refrigerated section, often by the butter, of your grocery store.)

5 lg. Granny Smith apples (green & tart)
1 C sugar
2 T. flour
1/4 t. salt
2 t. cinnamon
1/4 t. nutmeg
4 T. butter

Remove the apple skin with a knife and remove the core.

*The first time I tried to make this, I took out a "peeler" to peel the apples! Maybe I was just nervous—LOL! I was told back then that peelers only worked on potatoes and some vegetables; however, now that I watch all kinds of cooking shows, I have seen great chefs use a peeler. If you have television, watch some of these shows to see how easy it is and to get to know how to do more things around the kitchen!

Slice the apples very thin for more flavor and tenderness. Mix all of the five dry ingredients together. Follow the directions on the piecrust box to prepare the crust.

Layer apples along the bottom of the crust, and sprinkle the dry mixture over each layer until all the dry mixture covers all the apples. (The first time I did this, I sprinkled the mixture on like I sprinkle sugar on my children's cereal—sparingly. My friend laughed and told me that I had to get *all of it* over the apples—well, then I understood.) Now put the four sliced tablespoons of butter on top of the apples and cover with the top crust, then pinch together. Put slits in the top crust and paint with milk to make the crust shine. Bake in preheated 400° oven for 50 minutes.

My daughter, Tyler, made dozens of pies while we lived on our farm using the Jonathan apples from our tree. We took them out in the morning to thaw and baked them the usual way. They were absolutely wonderful—even the ones that were more than a year old, after we moved, were delicious!

French Apple Pie

For French Apple, just leave the top crust off and spread the cinnamon mixture from the "Overnight Coffee Cake" recipe (below). Bake for the same time and temperature as the pie above.

Cobblers

I keep pre-made piecrusts (see above) on hand in my freezer and some pie filling (in cans) in my pantry. Just flour the pre-made crust well and place in a pie pan. Now pour a can of pie filling in the middle, and pull up the sides to "try" and pinch it closed, covering the top (leave a little hole). Sprinkle with sugar (and cinnamon if it's apple filling) and bake in a preheated 400° oven for 20–30 minutes. Scoop and serve hot with vanilla ice cream—easy and delicious!

**This is a great recipe to teach young girls to make because it is so easy and fairly foolproof.

Cookies!!

Cookies are my family's *favorite* dessert. My ex-husband used to be our cookie baker, and then I took over. Next my oldest daughter took over baking our cookies and quickly became our most famous and requested baker. Then my second daughter had this job until recently when my youngest daughter, who began baking at 10-years-old, took the job and loves it! Many evenings she is asked by everyone to "make cookies tonight—*ppplllease!*"

As I said earlier, cookies or the cobbler seems to be the best way to teach your daughter to cook. Always begin with baking since it is easier to mix and bake something than it is to have to regulate a burner or a flame. But I think the key reason this works so well is because just about everyone loves homemade sweets; therefore, your daughter instantly gets rave responses (if she doesn't, make sure you tell your family to "make a fuss," if they ever want homemade baked goods again!). This gives her the confidence and motivation to learn to bake more (to get the attention and compliments), which will lead to also being a great cook!

Cookie Tips

Melted butter: Microwave your butter for all of your cookie recipes, while you get your ingredients out. My ex-husband used to let the butter sit out and cream the way he saw his grandmother and mother do. Since my mother didn't bake, I never knew any better, so I microwaved mine until the butter was melted. Everyone raved about my cookies, so I taught my daughter to do the same thing. In our microwave, it takes one minute for each stick.

Organizing your ingredients: Ladies, I put all my ingredients out in a row along the counter according to the order of use (left to right). After I measure and put it in the bowl, I put the container back. This is not only a good method for keeping your kitchen clean, but it also helps me to remember what I have already added, since I am usually interrupted at least a dozen times when I am trying to concentrate.

I also do this when I'm getting ready in the morning and putting on my make-up, since I am always "thinking of something." Prior to this method, I would forget to wear deodorant or look in the mirror hours after getting dressed only to notice I forgot to put on mascara!

Some more baking secrets:

• When baking cookies, bake only one pan at a time and turn it when they are halfway through baking, unless some like the cookies crispy then leave it the same way for a variety of doneness (crispier will be in the back of the oven).

• My girls also drop the pan to get the cookies to "fall" that make the cookies chewier.

• Also, let the sheet cool before putting more dough on it. If you put the dough on a hot cookie sheet, they will spread out and very thin.

• Make an investment in a **metal** cookie scooper to have evenly baked cookies that are easier and faster to make. Metal scoopers may be hard to find, but well worth the hunt.

The Easiest Cookies Ever

My youngest daughter wanted desperately to bake, but I thought was a bit too young, then I found this recipe that proved to launch her into becoming an extremely talented baker!

1 box cake mix
1/3 C oil
2 eggs
powdered/confectioner's sugar

Preheat oven to 350° then stir (by hand) dry cake mix, oil, and eggs in a large bowl until dough ball forms. Dust hands with sugar and shape into 1inch balls. Roll balls into sugar and place 2 inches apart on ungreased cookie sheets.

Bake 8-10 minutes or until center is set, not gooey. Remove from pans after setting about a minute and cool on wire racks.
• Macy made chocolate crinkles first by using a dark chocolate cake mix.

• Next she made Snicker Doodles by using a yellow cake mix and rolling them in cinnamon sugar.

The possibilities are endless, and so are the compliments she received. One of her older brothers was thrilled to take a bag of these to work to share with his coworkers who could not believe that his 10-year-old sister made them!

Once your daughter has mastered these, then it is an easy step to the rest of the cookie recipes!

Extraordinary Chocolate Chip Cookies

No matter how great your chocolate chip cookies are, they can never match this recipe! My brother, who is a professor in Japan, requests these cookies within minutes after stepping through our front door when he visits.

I am going to give you the double, double batch measurements that we use. Allow everyone to get "their fill" as they are coming out of the oven. Then fill the "cooled" cookies in an airtight container and freeze the rest.

When company comes, or someone just "drops by," take these (and any other kinds of cookies you make) out of your freezer and put them on a plate. Make some great coffee or a pot of tea, and by the time the coffee is done, the cookies are thawed to serve to delighted guests!

Mix in medium microwaveable bowl:
2 sticks of butter, melted 2 min. in microwave
1 C Crisco
1-1/2 C sugar

1-1/2 C brown sugar
2 t. vanilla

---

mix in big bowl:
4-1/2 C flour
2 t. baking soda
2 t. salt

Pour dry into wet ingredients and add four eggs then two bags (or four cups) chocolate chips. Bake at 375° for 9–11 minutes.

Peanut Butter Cookies

I know. I sound like a broken record when I tell you how delicious something is, but these are the best peanut butter cookies I've ever eaten. The secret is that you use "chunky" peanut butter!

Mix in medium microwaveable bowl:
1 C (2 sticks) butter, melted
1 C chunky peanut butter
1 C sugar
1 C brown sugar

Add:
2 eggs and 1 t. vanilla

Mix in smaller bowl:
2-1/2 C flour
1 t. baking powder
1-1/2 t. baking soda
1/2 t. salt

Combine both bowls

CHILL IN REFRIGERATOR FOR THREE HOURS

Scoop and roll in sugar. Press down with a fork making a criss-cross pattern. Bake at 375° for 10–12 minutes.

Chewy Toffee Rancher Cookies

You will find that these are the best cookies you've ever eaten, guaranteed! Unfortunately, we had a run of guests that begged us to make them and we "over-dosed" on them.

Mix in medium bowl:
1 C shortening
1 C sugar
1 C brown sugar

Add 3 eggs

Mix in small bowl:
2 C flour
1/2 t. salt
1/2 t. baking powder
1 t. soda
1 t. vanilla
2 C oats
2 C corn flakes

1-1/2 packages of English Toffee bits (10 oz. bag)

Mix dry, mix moist, combine, then add toffee bits.

Bake on WELL-GREASED cookie sheet at 350° for 10 minutes. Make sure they are dark on the edges; if they are underdone they really are no good. Cool on wire rack before eating for best flavor.

Note: Your spatula will stick when removing the cookies from the sheet. So, after removing three cookies, wipe off the end of the spatula with a moist cloth.

Oatmeal Crinkles

You have never in your life tasted cookies like these. Last year, our pastor announced how much he loved oatmeal cookies. Every one of my children leaned forward in the pew to motion to me that I needed to bring him some of mine! Isn't it nice to have fans?

Mix in medium microwaveable bowl:
4 sticks of butter, melted
4 C sugar
4 eggs
2 t. vanilla

Mix in small bowl:
2 C oats
2 C raisins (optional)
5-1/2 C flour
3 t. soda
1/2 t. salt

Combine both bowls. Roll into a ball and then roll into 2/3 cups sugar. Bake in preheated 350° oven for 15 minutes until they puff and are lightly browned.

Chocolate Fudge Cake

This chocolate cake recipe, with the following icing recipe, is the most delicious cake you have ever tasted. For a fancier cake (this is what I do for my friends' birthday cakes), spread the first (or bottom) layer with raspberry preserves, then the icing. Incredible!!!

I will warn you that it is very heavy and rich. Normally I use a box cake mix with the icing recipe below.

3 C flour (take out 6 T.)
1-1/2 t. baking soda
3/4 t. salt (1/2 & 1/4 t.)
3/4 C butter (1-1/2 sticks)
2-1/4 C sugar
1-1/2 t. vanilla
3 eggs
3 (1 oz.) squares unsweetened baking chocolate, melted
1-1/2 C ice water

Preheat oven to 350°. Generously grease and flour three (nine inch) round cake pans. Sift the flour, baking soda, and salt into a medium-sized bowl. Cream butter in a large bowl; then, gradually add sugar and vanilla, and beat until mixture is fluffy.

Add eggs, one at a time, beating well after each. Blend in melted chocolate. Now, add the dry ingredients alternating with ice water. Mix the batter for two minutes. Pour into greased and floured pans.

Bake in preheated oven for 30–35 minutes or until wooden toothpick comes out clean. Cool in pans on a wire rack for 10 minutes. Then, remove from pans and cool completely.

The LIGHTEST Frosting

When my friends have a party, they ask me to bring my cake as their "birthday present"!

1/3 C powdered sugar
1 box (3-1/2 oz.) instant vanilla pudding
3/4 C cold milk
8 oz. tub of Cool Whip (I have tried, unsuccessfully to use real whipping cream but if you ever master it, please send me the recipe!)

Keep everything very cold by putting your bowl and beaters in the freezer. Mix the top three ingredients on high speed for about two minutes until thick. Carefully fold in Cool Whip with a rubber spatula. That's it!

For more variety, use different flavors of pudding mix with different kinds of cake mixes and get creative. Our last birthday, Tara's, I used fresh strawberries and used the juice (after slicing thinly, cover them with sugar and refrigerate) as the liquid in the cake, and in place of the milk. Then I spread the strawberries in the middle and over the top and sides. Not only delicious, but impressive!

Tasty Gingerbread

My mother tells me that she was known for delicious gingerbread, but somehow lost the recipe. She says that this is just as delicious as hers, but she still liked to tell me the story of how she used to make hers in a cast iron skillet whenever I made her some of my gingerbread.

This can be served as a dessert, a tasty breakfast treat, or as a snack. Amazingly delicious!

1 stick butter
3/4 C firmly packed brown sugar
1 egg, beaten
1/2 C light molasses
1 C milk
2-1/2 C flour
1/2 t. salt
1 t. baking powder
1 t. baking soda
1 t. ground ginger
1 t. cinnamon
Sugar for the top

Preheat oven to 375°. Generously grease a nine inch square baking dish. Cream the butter and sugar. Add egg, molasses, and milk; beat until well blended. Sift in flour, salt, soda, powder, ginger, and cinnamon. Beat until mixed. Pour into greased pan, sprinkle with sugar, and bake in preheated oven for about 30 minutes or until wooden pick comes out clean. Serve slightly warm or at room temperature.

Sweet Cornbread

This recipe is not from the South. In the South, the cornbread is not sweet at all and is baked in cast iron skillets (I have never acquired a taste for southern cornbread). However, you will not believe how delicious this northern sweet cornbread is. It is so tasty that if there is ever any left over, it is eaten up the next morning by the first man (or woman) up!

1 C flour
1 C cornmeal
1/2 C sugar
4 t. baking powder
3/4 t. salt
2 eggs, slightly beaten
1 C milk
1 stick butter
1/2 C sweet frozen corn

Preheat oven to 425°. Generously grease a nine inch square pan. In a medium bowl, combine flour, cornmeal, sugar, powder, and salt. Add eggs, milk, and butter. Mix only until well blended. Put into greased pan. Bake in preheated oven 20–25 minutes or until the wooden stick comes out clean, and the top is lightly browned. Serve warm.

If you need to double the recipe, you can mix them together, but bake them in two nine inch square pans, so that they will cook in the center.

This can be eaten as a dessert—it is so good; however, we usually eat it with our fried chicken dinner and our chili.

Equivalent Measurements

3 teaspoons	=	1 tablespoon
4 tablespoons	=	1/4 cup
8 tablespoons	=	1/2 cup
12 tablespoons	=	3/4 cup
16 tablespoons	=	1 cup

Liquid Measures

2 tablespoons	=	1 ounce
2 ounces	=	1/4 cup
4 ounces	=	1/2 cup
6 ounces	=	3/4 cup
8 ounces	=	1 cup
2 cups	=	1 pint
4 cups	=	1 quart

Dry Measurements

4 ounces	=	1/4 pound
8 ounces	=	1/2 pound
12 ounces	=	3/4 pound
16 ounces	=	1 pound

—————— Chapter 14 ——————

Making the Most of

Fast and Easy Meals

Meals that Work So You Don't Have To!

> She rises also while it is still night,
> And gives food to her household,
> And portions to her maidens.
> —Proverbs 31:15

As we become organized in our homes and try to stay two steps ahead, instead of five steps behind, some days are still hectic; therefore, easy meals are a must. Having been the mother of seven and feeding a family of nine, I always needed to plan ahead and be creative.

Even though there are just five children and myself at home now, I now tend to feed even more—my children and all their friends!

When I married I couldn't cook at all. I only became a better cook when I decided to humble myself. "Humble yourselves, therefore, under the mighty hand of God, that He may exalt you at the proper time, casting all your anxiety upon Him, because He cares for you" (1 Pet. 5:6–7).

When my husband left me in 1989, I told the ladies in the classes I taught that I simply couldn't cook. That week a friend told me that she would come over and help me make a delicious and "easy" pie. "Easy" was the word I was looking for. She came over and step-by-step she walked me through the pie recipe in the previous chapter. It was God doing a new thing in my life!

Soon, many ladies began giving me recipes with the word "easy" in the title, and I was off and running. Now, I want to share some of my easiest meals with you that are sure to please.

Microwave Ham Steak

One of the easiest meals ever is a Ham Steak. I buy a ham, ask the meat department to slice 1/2 of the ham (starting at the rounded side) in thin slices (ask for "shaved," which is even better), and leave 1/2 for me to slice thick. This gives me meat for sandwiches and a dinner for my family.

I pour the juice from a can of pineapple chunks into a microwave safe dish and put into it the thick slices of ham to cook for about 1/2 minute. The first slices are for the youngest, so they will be cool when the last slice is cooked. I serve it with pineapple chunks over the meat, dinner rolls, and a vegetable. This whole meal takes only 10–15 minutes to make!

Nachos

I always keep COOKED ground beef in the freezer, and then thaw a little in the microwave whenever I need it. If you cook ground beef when you get home, it tastes so fresh AND it can be used for many quick and easy meals.

For nachos, add a package of taco seasoning or add your own seasoning. Place corn tortilla chips on a cookie sheet, pour the taco meat, and shredded cheese over the top, and cook under the broiler. I serve it with salsa for dipping, and we all sit around the table and enjoy a tasty, fun meal.

Dallas Chicken

The name for this meal was derived from my son, Dallas, who was able to make this at five-years-old while I was nursing his brother, Easton.

Take boneless, skinless chicken breasts and cut into bite-size pieces (I did this step!). Then, put one can of cream of chicken soup and one small container of sour cream in a baking dish and stir. Now, stir in the chicken pieces and cook about an hour at 325°. Serve over rice, noodles, or baked potato with a vegetable. Simple and delicious!

Surprise Quiche

I always keep the frozen, already prepared piecrust, on hand for cobblers and quiches.

Whenever you have left over meat, cheese, or vegetables—you can make a quick, easy, and delicious meal! California restaurants charge six dollars a slice for the strangest combinations of ingredients in their quiches—so be creative!

Simply cut up all your ingredients and put into a prepared piecrust. Beat four eggs with a little milk and pour over the top and bake until the middle of the egg is cooked. 425° for 15 min., reduce to 300° for another 15 min., and then sit for another 10 min. Serve with rolls and a salad.

Loaded Baked Potato

Cook your potatoes in the microwave. Put them in a circle, cook for 5 minutes, then pierce them again with a fork to check for tenderness. Continue to cook at 5 min. (or less) intervals until all are tender.

Then, if you like the skins crispier transfer them to your oven for about 10 minutes, while you get the other ingredients together. Get out your leftover meats, vegetables, cheeses, sour cream, and bacon bits to put over your potato. It's better, and a lot cheaper, than any restaurant that serves the same thing!

Southern Fried Chicken

My next-door neighbor gave me her secret family recipe that she was famous for. Though she used regular chicken cut up, I use boneless, skinless chicken. Dip the chicken in buttermilk and then in self-rising flour that has salt and pepper added. Fry on pretty high heat in peanut oil (just don't let it burn). The meat is so juicy and tasty—even skinless!

Pork Chops

My mother, bless her heart, could not cook, but **everyone** loved her pork chops (if you didn't mind that they were burnt). Her secret was to sprinkle seasoned salt over each chop, roll it in flour, and fry in oil. I now buy the boneless chops that have less fat and tend to be thicker and juicier. Serve them with applesauce for the true McGovern way (that was my maiden name).

Enchiladas

If you mix your cooked ground beef or canned chicken in with your favorite taco sauce and a little water or with salsa, your meat is ready to go—all you need to do is assemble the enchiladas.

Heat the corn tortillas in the microwave to make them soft, put in your meat, and roll. Cover with canned enchilada sauce, sprinkle with cheese, and bake about 15 minutes at 350°.

Enchiladas go well with refried beans (in a can) and tortilla chips. If you like Spanish rice, cook white rice with the juice from stewed tomatoes and a little salt and pepper.

My Family's *Favorite* Meals

Tuna Fish Cakes

This was a recipe my mother used to make and is similar to more expensive crab cakes. My children actually go wild over these.

Use the tuna packed in oil, dice up some onion (you can use a food processor for this), and add one raw egg per big can of tuna (this holds the tuna and onion together). Mix it up early in the day. If you want the easy method, fry them on a griddle, but the *tastiest* way is to fry them in oil (they do splatter and pop occasionally, so be careful).

Use a medium-sized cookie scooper to get the right size. Flatten them out like burgers (you can call them Tuna Burgers if you prefer), and fry them until they are browned on each side. We serve them with elbow macaroni, and prepare a sauce with a can of tomato soup with a little bit of water. The sauce can go over both, or just the noodles, to suit the individual's taste.

Chicken Pot Pie

Use any chicken meat you'd like to fill the bottom of the pan you plan to use. I used to boil boneless chicken in bouillon, and cool before breaking apart. After Y2K, I had at my disposal a lifetime supply of canned chicken and turkey meat (actually it lasted almost five years!).

Heat a can of cream of chicken soup mixed with just a little milk (about 1/4 of a can) in a pan, and pour it into a microwavable dish.

Throw in some mixed vegetables (you can add potato chunks too if they are diced small) and the chicken, and cover the mixture with a refrigerated piecrust (if you prefer more crust, you can cover the bottom with another crust). Cut slits in the top for the steam to escape, and bake in a 425° oven for 30 minutes or until the crust is a light brown.

Roast Beef

A roast is nothing new, but let me encourage you to put yours into a crock-pot with your seasoning (we use dried onion soup mix). You can have it cooking while you are at church. If you put it in frozen, make sure it is at the highest setting), and if you plan to use a cheap, less fatty roast, make sure you put it in the night before church.

Put potatoes in your oven to bake on low about 325°. When your family gets back from church, you can have an afternoon dinner ready by the time they change their clothes and sit down at your (already set) table.

Gravy

A roast is normally dry and uninteresting without gravy, at least for most men. My ex-husband was a big gravy fan and my children inherited this preference. I had tried to pick up my mother's technique; however, as Providence would have it, I never learned. The fact was, her gravy, though smooth, had very little flavor because she used milk as the liquid.

One night, years ago, we were invited to a dinner given at the church for all recent newcomers. It was a small church, and the older ladies put this occasion on periodically to welcome new families. On the menu was a roast with mashed potatoes and GRAVY. My ex-husband was in heaven! Not only was the meat tender, but the gravy was out of this world! My ex mentioned to our server that if he hadn't already been married, he would marry the person who made this delicious gravy.

When the meal was done, a kind, older gentleman stepped up to him and announced, "I heard that you wanted to marry me!" My ex-husband was startled until the man continued, "I made the gravy!" Though he didn't marry this man, LOL (laugh out loud), he did marry, but I still make the gravy!!

Here is the recipe that is easy and always delicious, no matter what meat you are serving!

When your meat is cooking, pour water into a glass jar or Tupperware container with a tight lid. Put some flour into it and shake until it resembles milk. For richer gravy, use more flour with the water so it looks like thick cream. For milder gravy, put only enough flour in for it to resemble non-fat milk. Now, pour your meat drippings into a saucepan and bring to boil.

With a whisk, begin whisking the boiling meat juices, and slowly pour in the flour and water combination. Go slowly, and watch for your family's desired thickness, then stop. Remember, you can always add flour/water to make it thicker, so be careful not to add too much to the juices.

If you are short on meat drippings, make your gravy thinner, by adding LESS flour/water, so that it will stretch. I prefer the thinner gravy since it has more flavor!

Easy Lasagna

The trick to making it easy is by not having to cook the noodles! To accomplish this, simply use twice as much sauce as usual and make sure each noodle is heavily coated with sauce. Also, make it ahead of time so it can sit for a couple of hours before baking.

1 pkg. lasagna noodles
2 jars of your family's favorite sauce
1 small container ricotta cheese
2 pkg. mozzarella cheese
Parmesan cheese

Mix ricotta and one package of mozzarella cheese together. You can season the cheese with garlic or mix in a little spinach if you'd like, but my family prefers it just plain. Pour enough sauce to cover a long casserole dish. Spread out three noodles and pour sauce on top (if the noodles aren't cooked, turn them over and coat the other side).

Now, spread 1/2 of the cheese mixture on top of the noodles. Lay another row of three noodles on top and cover generously with sauce (again on both sides if the noodles aren't cooked). Spread the remaining 1/2 of the mixture on top of the noodles and lay one more row of three noodles on top, and cover generously with sauce; flip over and pour more sauce on top so that both sides are coated. Finish up with the remaining package of mozzarella cheese, and sprinkle Parmesan cheese over the top of the cheese. Cover with foil and bake at 350° for 45 minutes, remove the foil and bake another 10 minutes until the cheese is browned. Let it sit for 15 minutes while you whip up a salad!

Just recently my son's fiancé told me her mother had pulled her back out, so I offered to bring her a dinner to help. She told me when I picked up my pan that everyone, including all her picky eaters,

LOVED this simple recipe and ate it all. Isn't that what it's all about? Thank you Lord!

Meatloaves

There are so many ways to create diversity in your meatloaves. Let me share one of mine with you then let your creative juices flow to develop some new creations of your own. Mexican meatloaf is a favorite with my family. Use the crumbs from your taco chips (you can use flavored ones too) to replace the breadcrumbs. Use taco sauce to replace the ketchup and taco mix to replace the seasoning (just be careful of too much seasoning!). Serve it with rice, beans, and tortilla chips.

By changing the mold you use, you can spark your family's enthusiasm. Use two pie pans, and the meat loaf can be cut into pie slices. Scoop your mashed potatoes out with an ice cream scooper and it'll look like pie a la mode. Fun and easy!

Thick Beef Stew

Stew is simply using stew meat or cutting up a cheaper roast. I have cooked it many ways, but during a crisis, when I forgot to put it on early in the crock-pot, I found the tastiest way with the most-tender meat.

Cut your meat up in tinier pieces—more like tiny bite-size. Cut your potatoes up small too. Then place both the meat and potatoes in a pan, cover with water over them about an inch, and add seasoning (we also use the onion soup mix for ease and flavor my family will all eat). Bring to a boil and boil it until the meat is tender and the corners of the potatoes are rounded and smooth.

Just minutes before serving add your vegetables. Frozen vegetables take just minutes (since they are blanched before they are frozen) and they stay fresh a bit longer. Canned are already tender, so just put them in long enough to heat.

If you like your stew *thick*, listen to this. My mother used to "flour and fry" her meat before cooking it in the stew like most women do.

Since I liked to use my crock-pot, I did away with this step. However, I was unable to duplicate the thick gravy, and my family, especially my boys, pleaded for gravy. I prayed and found another way—voila, gravy!

When your stew is done, about 10–15 minutes before you serve, simply mix up the flour and water in the jar (see the gravy recipe above). While stirring the stew, slowly pour the flour and water into your stew until it has your desired thickness; then taste. You may have to add a bit more seasoning to regain the flavor.

Crock Pot Recipes

Chicken Parmesan

Put your favorite spaghetti sauce (with a little water) in the crock-pot with some boneless chicken breasts and/or thighs. Cook all day. Make pasta and a vegetable (summer squash or zucchini is delicious with this). Then put one breast or thigh over the pasta with the sauce, and sprinkle it with Parmesan cheese. Yum!

Crock-Pot Beef Stew

Your boys will love your stew, if you tell them it's what the cowboys ate! Put in stew meat and any leftover or frozen vegetables you have lying around. Add seasoning (I use Lipton onion soup mix). Cook all day and serve with rolls or bread (like the cowboys). To vary this, I make thick stew by adding flour mixed with water—shake it in a Tupperware container or jar (see Thick Beef Stew above). Also, you can add stewed tomatoes and beans for variety and extra nutrition.

Bar-B-Q Sandwiches

One of our favorite places to eat bar-b-q had incredible chopped beef sandwiches. My ex-husband commented that it tasted like Cattleman's (you can use any brand of bar-b-q sauce you like). I put stew meat in the crock-pot and pour the sauce over it and cook it all day. At the end of the day, don't pour off the water, just break apart the meat with a wooden spoon and add more sauce if you'd like. Serve on a hamburger bun or Texas Toast.

Another favorite is when I use this same recipe, but use boneless chicken breasts instead of stew meat. Both of these are good enough to serve to guests.

More Recipes

Asking for recipes from your friends is the best way to find great meals and to give them your friends the riches of a true compliment. If you don't know how to cook, do what I did—humble yourself and ask for help.

Be sure to watch some cooking shows for inspiration. Many of the shows now are geared to women who were not trained to cook, many by women who learned by doing rather than being chefs themselves.

If you love a particular kind of meal, and don't know how to make it, then try going to this website that I recently found.

www.recipezaar.com

One day I was busy trying to cook (I believe I had a houseful of refugees from an ice storm) and my sister demanded that I come up with a meal for the director of her assisted living home where she lives. Her director woman had attended one of my seminars for "once a month meal planning" (from chapter 10) and decided to ask each of the residents to come up with *two* of their favorite meals to be made each month. Brilliant idea!

My sister and I decided that Mexican was her favorite, and a tortilla soup would make a dinner special. So I went online to find a recipe and "stumbled" on the above site in an answer to my prayer.

What I like best about the site are the ratings (one to five stars) and the reviews (be sure to set your "find" by the ratings). I read all the reviews (after I sort by the ratings; sticking to five stars) so I know WHY people like the recipe (in case it is exactly why my family wouldn't like it).

The other great thing about this site is that you can create the recipe for the amount of people you serve (by changing the serving size on the top right), and it gives you the ability to print a recipe off easily.

There are also many other options you will find on the left side of the site such as: Add to Cook Book, Add to Meal Plan, Add to Shopping List, and Add to Menu. Go take a look and see if it helps!

Some day I may take the time to post all my meals to share with others or is this a just a pipedream? (Pipedream is defined as an "unrealistic notion: a goal, hope, or plan so fanciful that it is very unlikely to be realized.)

Chapter 15

Making the Most of

Clothing

Buying and Washing Clothes

> . . . they were not in want;
> Their clothes did not wear out . . .
> —Nehemiah 9:21

Clothes are very expensive to buy and/or replace if they are stained, ruined or in ill repair. It is, therefore, very important to keep your family looking like "children of the King" by keeping their clothes clean and in good repair. Even if you if you are struggling financially, you can usually dress well with so many yard sales and thrift stores available nowadays.

Even if you are a one-income family or are divorced, you have this promise, that "she who remains at home will divide the spoil"! (Ps. 68:12).

Even if you are unable to afford garage sales or thrift stores, there are so many families who are just "looking" for someone who can wear their children's outgrown clothes—so make your needs known. First make it known to God about your needs through prayer. God tells us that HE will supply all your needs, but He wants you to ask Him.

Secondly, make your need for clothing known by mentioning it to someone who clearly is "through" having children and has children just a bit bigger than your own. A friend of mine told me a wonderful example of this. She had always admired a friend's little girl who wore the most gorgeous designer clothing. She simply asked her friend what she did with the outgrown clothes. The mother now passes all her daughter's clothing onto this friend who has six children.

When I was "delivered" from having yard sales or trying to make a buck by selling our clothes to consignment shops (as I said in an earlier chapter), our family began overflowing with clothing! It took me a long time of prayer before I found a group at our church that passes clothing around so I could pass Macy's clothing to them. Our neighbor just mentioned to me that she loves "hand me downs" that was such a blessing for me. I *never* even thought of giving her Cooper's clothes that he has outgrown! So be sure to ASK. The rest of our clothes, I simply give to the closest thrift store to our home. I make it simple by putting a silver trash can with a black drawstring bag in it marked "Give Away" so that anytime we no longer want something, it can go right in the bag and onto the thrift store.

Whether you need clothes, or you have clothes to give away, it is important that you keep your clothes clean, which is what this chapter is all about!

Before I get started, however, I want to share my heart regarding mothers who have their children do their "own" clothes. I am all for training my children (as you know from my workbook *A Wise Woman*), but I am not in favor of this system, because I like *living* and promoting "family." Though our children learn to cook, clean, and do laundry, we do not do it "independently" from each other, but rather we learn to do it as a family.

Society as a whole loves to "divide and conquer" yet our very nature draws us to wanting to "belong." Cults prey on young people, because they are "communal" and these young people finally feel they are needed (even if it is trying to sell beads at an airport!). I am not saying that if your children do their own laundry they will end up a member of a cult, I just want to emphasis promoting family and "servanthood" (caring for each other rather than "self") that is becoming as outdated as remaining a virgin before marriage. Okay, enough, moving on . . .

Praise God. If you have a washer and dryer, PRAISE God for your modern conveniences! If you don't have to wash on a board, at a river, or carry water and boil it, praise the Lord! Most of us in the United States don't *have to* hang out our wash to dry, but have a clothes drier! Traveling around the world proved how blessed we are since most countries hang their clothes out to dry! We don't have to load coals in our iron when pressing our clothes either!

Be thankful. Be thankful by showing God your appreciation for the clothes you have by:

1. Keeping them clean: Use bibs, aprons, and a stain remover when you or your family does spill.

2. Keeping them wrinkle free: Keep up with your ironing, and fold or hang as soon as the drier stops. Also, not overloading your washer and drier will help with the wrinkles.

3. Keeping them mended: A stitch in time really does save nine! Learn to hand sew or keep your sewing machine set up with white thread during the warm months and black thread during the colder months for quick mending. If you know how to sew, but don't have a machine, there are very small machines, even hand held ones, that will mend a seam or tear.

Diligence. Setting a washday schedule and a routine will increase productivity and keep you from dreading this very important job you do for your family.

1. Sort your clothes by using three different-colored baskets: use a white basket for whites, a light color for your lights or bright clothing, and a dark basket for your darks. Teach young children their colors by having them sort their own clothes as they take them off. Once they are either dressed in their bedclothes or dressed for the day, they can be trained to bring their soiled clothes to the laundry room. If you prefer, you can have a laundry basket in each room for them to bring to you on laundry day. However, very often children will throw *clean* clothes that they try on and don't wear or put dirty clothes in their drawers that you discover a week later. If you have either of these situations, you might want to use the first method.

2. Set days, i.e., Monday, Wednesday, Friday, for your washdays, or you can wash a load as soon as that colored basket is full. (If you like this method, make sure you have your family sort their own clothes as they take them off). This works better for smaller families, where set washdays are a **must** for larger families. Recently I was blessed with one of those front load washers that does 17 pair of jeans! Now I have just ONE washday a week, not counting another day for towels and sheets that my 13-year-old son does.

3. Turn the clothes the right way out or inside out for sweaters, girl's tights, or other items you want to protect. Teach your children to do this themselves. If my children don't turn their clothes, I make a pile of all the clothes that are unturned and make one child (the biggest culprit) to turn or shake out the rest of the family's socks. It only takes ONE time for each child to turn someone else's socks (or underwear) for them to remember to turn their own clothes!

4. If you zip up your clothes, they will fold easier, but more important, it saves the life of your clothing. A zipper frays clothing in the washer and especially in the drier.

5. Take time to look for soiled or stained clothing, and pre-treat them with a stain stick, or what I prefer is the new liquid detergent I use that gets out **everything**, including blood!

6. Ooops, I spoke too soon. The only thing my new laundry detergent doesn't get out is anything oily or greasy. For this I use "Goo Gone." If you can't find this, look or ask for a citrus stain remover that gets out gum. It took out a stain from a baby romper that was **covered** with red lipstick in just two washings! When my sister visited, she just about cried when she told me her son (who had *begged* his mom for a pair of designer shorts for the summer) got a black oil stain on it. She told me she had tried "everything" and it didn't help at all. It took two washings with "Goo Gone." Just make sure you cover the stain, let it dry, then use a liquid detergent or stain stick on it when you wash (it explains it in the directions).

7. My favorite laundry detergent is OUR Detergent. It's a liquid, which is what I always use with my darks, since I often end up with powder marks on dark colors. It uses a pump, so you don't have messy cups. It works with cold water. It gets my clothes so white, and the colors are so much brighter. I found out about it from a Christian woman's magazine, and I have told everyone about it. You can order online at www.ourproductsonline.com. Recently, a neighbor I recommended the OUR detergent to asked what I thought of their other cleaning products, which I had not tried. After trying them, I now love most their products, especially their powdered whitener. Their products are safe for your skin, without petroleum byproducts or harmful chemicals that you don't want to use next to your family's skin. And if that is not enough to convince you to try this, I figured that it cost my family of nine just $5.00 a month to use! Now with my front load washer I use half a pump or $2.50 a month. I use the smallest recommended amount per wash and still cannot believe the great results and such a cheap price! If you do give this product a try, mention my name and they will send me money toward more of their products! Thanks!!

Washing Tips:

1. If you want to stay ahead of the game, collect and sort your clothes at night and start your first wash load—whites. If you do your whites at night, you save competing with the hot water you use for showers in the morning.

2. Throw your whites, which consist mostly of towels, underwear, and socks in the drier since these will sit before folding. When you wake up, you have a load to fold, your third load in the washer, and your second load going in the drier. This saves me so much time it is unbelievable!

3. To get **cleaner** clothes, don't over fill your washer.

4. Use a detergent that requires only a quarter cup. Others have fillers, which can burn clothes, cause skin irritation on children, and other family members that have sensitive skin,

and may be the cause of sickness and diseases like autoimmune disorders. Again, I highly recommend trying OUR detergent.

5. Though I used to use liquid fabric softener and recommended using a Downy Ball in previous editions of this book, I no longer recommend using chemicals that come in contact with the skin that are easily absorbed into the body. **Fabric sheets are said to be one of the worst products you can use regarding your health, and often cause skin rashes.** A natural softener, especially for towels, is vinegar. There are different kinds, but Heinz makes a good one that is made from vegetables, not petroleum, and vinegar is so cheap to use. For a nice scent, I use natural lemon extract that you can get for about $5 in a health food store. You use just about 4-5 drops for a fresh scent.

6. For clothes that you do not want to go into the drier, put these in a net laundry bag. All my children know that a net laundry bag does not go in the drier. Before I discovered this method I had so many articles of clothing that would be ruined by drying. It is the drier, not the washer, that makes clothes wear out and fades the colors. So now most of my own clothes are hung up after I put them on an "air only" cycle to fluff them and get out some of the wrinkles.

Drying Tips:

1. Remove your clothes immediately, fold or hang up, to eliminate wrinkles.

2. To save electricity—dry two small loads together.

3. Shake out clothes as you place them in the dryer, rather than throwing a giant wet ball of clothes, to get fewer wrinkles.

4. Place your laundry basket *under* the dryer door to prevent your clean clothes from falling on your dirty (or lint covered) laundry room (or garage) floor.

5. It is the dryer, not the washer, that fades colors, especially black items. So if you have something that you want to keep looking like new, don't dry it, but instead hang it up to dry. Then to help it get less stiff, put it in the drier for about 5 min. Just makes sure you don't forget it's in there! I set a timer so I don't forget.

6. My sister and I used to spray our jeans with a little water, or throw a wet washcloth in with them, so we didn't have to iron jeans or our wrinkled tops. I showed this trick to my 13-year-old daughter who thought it was the neatest thing she ever found! This works for just about any wrinkled item that you have that you don't need to look pressed.

Folding Tips:

The fastest way to fold is to have smaller baskets set aside for your:

1. towels and washcloths
2. socks
3. underwear

While folding, fill these baskets with your towels, socks, and underwear, until all your loads of laundry are done. Fold or hang up the remainder of the clothes immediately. My younger children fold these baskets for me (youngest the towels and washcloths to the oldest who folds the underwear), but before little helpers, sorting these items, and saving them to the end, cut *my* time folding.

When I fold a shirt or pair of pants, I hold them on the shoulders or at the waste band and give them a quick, sharp shake to smooth them out for a *quick* fold. There are some mothers who fold in a "fancy department store fashion" that forces them to have to do all the folding, since it is too complicate (or she is too picky) to have her family help.

My sister also likes them done in a "fancy" fashion that keeps her from keeping up with her folding! She never can get around to it (since it takes her probably five times as long as it takes me per load). So she buys more laundry baskets, lets them sit, and is then forced to iron everything before her family can wear it!

If your folding method causes you to fall into either of these groups, then find a simpler way. (Funny, while revising this chapter, I just so happened to be visiting my sister and folded at least a dozen or more loads to free up the laundry baskets. I had planned to buy some more for her until I found CLEAN clothes in baskets unfolded.)

To Reduce Ironing:

1. Hang up all your clothes immediately on colored plastic hangers (to be ironed if necessary).

2. Fold clothes right away, after *each* load to avoid wrinkles.

3. Fold underwear, socks, and towels after the *last* load.

4. Assign designated items to be folded by your children (youngest working up to the oldest).

    a. washcloths (youngest)
    b. towels
    c. underwear
    d. socks
    e. the rest of the clothes (oldest child or you)

"She looks well to the way of her
household and does not eat the bread of idleness"
—Proverbs 31:27

Putting Laundry Away:

1. Have the "folder" put away what he/she has folded into the proper drawers (if possible) or at least on the bed, dresser in the right room, or in designated laundry baskets that are taken to the room later once filled with all the loads.

2. You could have each child put away his/her own laundry. On

the farm, I used to make each family member take his or her own pile and then call out "laundry break." Each family member would take a "break" from whatever he or she was doing to come get his or her pile of laundry and put it away. It works great if you are all at home during the day.

3. On Mondays, or when a lot of clothes are in the wash, this is the best time to organize your drawers. You can put this task (to organize drawers) on your children's 3x5 cards for Monday. Then, the newly folded clothes can be added neatly to the newly organized drawers.

4. If you are short of drawer space, use colored, small baskets on shelves in your closets to organize your clothing, socks, underwear or shoes. This is especially helpful with small children's clothes. When my husband left us the first time, we had no dressers, so I found some cinder blocks and made shelves with boards. I found dollar plastic baskets, which served as our "dressers" for many years! I particularly liked being able to see all the clothes folded, not stuffed, in drawers.

5. Make sure you have a special drawer or basket for underwear, socks, nightclothes, shirts, pants and sweaters. Within the drawer or basket, divide it to separate socks from underwear or other smaller items. Shoeboxes work well in the sock and underwear drawer. I mention this because I was not raised this way. As a teenager, I believed I had "invented" this method of having a special drawer for different clothing items, not knowing that almost everyone lived like this!

6. Teach your children how to keep their drawers neat by having them sort their drawers each week as one of their task cards. It didn't take long for my older children to automatically put that card as "done," because they *learned* to **keep** their drawers organized!

Ironing Tips:

1. Ironing your husband's clothes shows other women in the workplace that "there is a woman who cares for this man"—

and one who is hard to compete with! If you want to keep him, don't have him iron his own clothes!!

2. Use a spray starch. It helps to keep clothes looking newer and crisper. You can buy liquid starch and put it into a spray bottle to save money, and it can be diluted to suit you or your husband's preference of crispness.

3. The proper order to iron a man's shirt is: collar, then cuffs, sleeves, left front, back then right front of his shirt.

4. Don't crowd clothes in the closet—get rid of what you don't wear! Rule of thumb—if you buy a dress, a shirt, or a pair of pants, **give one away.** Give to the poor—"Give and it shall be given!"

5. Use colored or matching hangers to make your closet look neat. Each of our family members has a specific color, which helps keep things in order in our laundry room and when putting away the items in rooms and in closets that are being shared. Colored hangers are extremely cheap. Use the little size for your younger children, and move up to the large hangers when things begin falling off the small hangers. The smaller children's hangers also work well for pants to keep the pants from sliding down to one end.

6. Collect all your *empty* hangers when you put away newly washed and ironed clothes. Have a place by your washer to hang the different colored hangers. Some places I have used are: a wire rack over my washer holds cleaning products on top and has a place to hang up hangers underneath; on the edge of a high table where I folded my clothes; and along the end of my ironing board. Now that I have a nice laundry room, I have a wooden bar along the top of my washer and drier. God is good isn't He?

7. Hang your clothes (in the closet) in some kind of order: all your shirts together, then pants, your dresses, next coats, and rearrange them with light to dark clothing within each section.

You may laugh, but it helps to find what you are looking for.

8. "Airing dirty laundry" is the biggest mistake you could make. Never share details of your husband, your child or friend's personal matters with others. "He who repeats a matter separates intimate friends" (Proverbs 17:9).

Stains:

1. The three most important things to remember are: always check for stains **before** putting items in the dryer (preferably before you put them into the wash basket); never iron over a stain; and use the easiest and least caustic method **first**.

2. Some of the stain sticks advertise to rub the stain before you put the item in the hamper. It has worked many times for me. If it doesn't work or you forget to use it, follow some of these other tips:

3. Fill your washer on low setting with soap and water (and the powdered OUR for whites), and put in the extra dirty or stained items to agitate alone. Then turn off the washer, and turn on a timer. Let the stained or soiled items soak for just 10 minutes. Check the stains again. Fill the washer the rest of the way, and then add the remaining laundry. This works for top-load washers only and is the only draw back to a front load washer.

4. If you have young children, you probably deal with a lot of stains. When I did, I usually washed my lights before I washed my whites, in case all my attempts still left a stain. At this point I use the more drastic method, and wash a light item with the whites. If this still doesn't work, go to the next step:

5. With extreme caution, use bleach with an old toothbrush, or better yet, purchase a bleach stick. It works great with white fabric, but if you must use it on a colored item, as soon as the stain disappears, run it under cold water to remove the bleach. If it's used on a colored item that would not come out, and it does get ruined, I figure that it was ruined anyway. So, if the

item gets damaged, or if the stain still doesn't come out, try this:

6. Seam rip a famous name label from another garment, and sew it over the stain or bleach mark. At the time this is being written, you find labels anywhere and everywhere on the garment. Many times it makes the article of clothing look more expensive! This also works for covering a small hole or tear. I have used a label to upgrade an inexpensive brand of clothing or the clothes I sew and women asked where I bought it!!

7. Use lingerie bags to wash panty hose, bras, knee high stockings, any delicate item or things you don't want to put in your drier. It not only protects them in the washer, but it also makes it easier to remember *not to put them in the dryer* where items with elastic lose their elasticity and bright colors lose their brilliance.

Chapter 16

Making the Most of

Sewing

Clever Sewing Notions

She stretches out her hands to the distaff,
And her hands grasp the spindle.
—Proverbs 31:19

Sewing is basically a "lost art" in today's society, but since Scripture tells us the "excellent wife" sews (well actually, she spins her own fabric, then she sews), I feel it must be important or God wouldn't have mentioned it! If you don't know how to sew at all, there are certainly women in your church with whom you can get together to learn the basics, like sewing on a button, hemming, mending, and operating a sewing machine. If you do sew, and sew fairly well, take a moment and ask the Lord to use you to help another woman learn, but first, do it in your own home.

Do you have daughters, or sons, who still don't know how to sew on a button? When a button is lost that article of clothing is worthless. So teaching how to do some basic sewing will benefit everyone. Parents send their children to school to learn so many things that they will never use in their future, but fail to teach them skills like sewing, cooking, cleaning and shopping that will help them all their lives.

For those of you who do sew, let's talk about some sewing tips that will help you save time and/or money. Most women don't think they have the time or that it is sometimes cheaper to buy it than sew it. Sometimes that is true; however, when I was left with four small children, the third being a girl, I found that sewing helped me to dress her in the kind of dresses I couldn't afford at the time. What helped me even more was that I had an outlet or hobby to do that kept my mind and hands busy when I was so terribly fearful of my future.

Tips to Save Time

Scissors. Put your scissors on a piece of elastic and hang them around your neck. I saw this being done at a fabric store by the personnel, and have done this for years! You never lose them. Do this for your crafts and if you plan to do a lot of gift-wrapping, like at Christmas time. It saves you so much time when you don't have to search for your scissors that have gotten under fabric or wrapping paper.

Pincushion. Use a wrist pincushion. You'll never end up at the sewing machine or ironing board without pins. It's even worse if they're hidden under a piece of material. (These first two tips cut my sewing time in half!)

Cutting patterns. Cut many patterns on one particular day, while you're all set up on the table or floor. Cut right over the V—then, go back and snip a quarter inch into each of the V's. This also saves time.

Patterns. Use the same pattern over and over. You'll know it so well it will cut down on the time of following the directions. You may even find short cuts to your pattern. Using different prints, solids, plaids and stripes, as well as various buttons and collars, will give each item a different look.

For patterns that you will use over and over again, make a pattern from a remnant of fabric. I did this for my daughter's dress pattern. It not only was easier to reuse than the thin paper pattern, it also did not require using pins to keep it in place for cutting! I was able to pass that pattern down and used it for my next two daughters.

Facings. Don't use the facings, instead line it—it is so much quicker! Just cut out the yoke of the garment doubled. You simply sew it around the neck and sleeves, turn and press! Using a different fabric print also adds to the look of your finished creation; this is what top designers do. They may use a totally different print and fabric, like hot pink with tiny polka dots in blue denim just to make it pop.

An entire child's wardrobe: Make a wardrobe for your toddler. Make two to four blouses or shirt in different styles (round collar, square collar, sailor collar, ruffle collar), then make different dresses or jumpsuits in various colors and slight pattern changes. This saved me so much money (when I didn't have any!) and got my children constant smiles of affection from strangers! The dresses I made for my oldest daughter actually went down through her two younger sisters and to my grand nieces!!

Bibs. Make and use bibs for little children (my four-year-olds still wore them when eating). This will save time with laundry and with having to buy new clothes! I also bought Battenburg collars at Wal-Mart in the fabric section for about five dollars, and use them with my daughters when we'd go out to eat. For my sons I made squared collars that were lined to go over their little rompers that not only saved their clothing, but also dressed up what they were wearing!

The first bib I made was from a remnant from a Christening gown I made with an old white towel for the backing. I also had some left over wide lace to go around the outside, and a wide satin ribbon for the ties. As I said before, each of my daughters wore this as a bib, but that's not all. When they turned about three years old, they would use it as a fancy apron when playing dress up! We still have that bib today in our memory chest. Was that thing anointed or what??

Tips for Saving Money

Buying patterns. Buy only one pattern for your boys and one for your girls. Make sure they have size variations (open the pattern before you buy it and look inside to see). I make a fabric pattern by cutting out the size I need on another piece of fabric I don't want. When you lay your fabric pattern on your good fabric, it will not need pins to hold it while you cut.

Lining. Use your unwanted white sheets for lining. You can also find white sheets at yard sales or at thrift stores, or use a complementing fabric to line. Also remember to use different fabric as a contrast: stripes inside your floral print are a nice combination. Keep your scraps of fabric for this purpose. Just lay what you have on top of your material to find a winning combination.

Buying fabric. Buy the fabric when it is a dollar a yard, no more than two dollars. You'll find fabric all over town this cheap if you look. When you need to sew something, check in your box of fabric first before rushing off to the store.

Avoid trendy. Buy the classic fabrics rather than the trendy. Also do this with your patterns. Then, the clothes can be passed down to other children without looking out of style.

Buttons can add style to your clothing at an inexpensive price. Many times Wal-Mart has buttons on sale for 10¢ or 25¢ cents a card. Different buttons, different trim, and different lengths of dresses make the clothes look different even though it is the same pattern.

Modest and warm: Make pantaloons for your girls—they are good to dress up an outfit, they are modest, and great for warmth in the winter.

Wear for years. Make your girl's dresses ballet length. Then, she can wear it the next year at calf length and the final year at the knee.

Teach your daughters to sew. As I said, there is no better way to help your daughters than to teach them skills that will help them when they are married. If you don't know how to sew, or cook, or do other domestic tasks, then find a woman who can train you and her. The "women's lib movement" left most of us unable to do simple tasks. This makes us struggle and dread everyday tasks that would be easily done had we learned when we were younger.

For more information on training your daughters (and your sons) for life when they leave home and get married, make sure you read *A Wise Woman* available for free on our website.

Suggested Reading

Clutter's Last Stand by Don Aslett. All of this man's books are wonderful, but this one is *must reading*. I kept jumping around this book looking for the quick tips for organizing, but there were none. I finally settled down and read the book from beginning to the end. It was enjoyable and funny, but most importantly, it changed the way I looked at what I owned. The unexpected side effect was that it changed my buying habits (I stopped buying what I didn't need). Check to see if this book is in your local library. Most bookstores carry it, or they can certainly order it for you.

Side-Tracked Home Executive by Pam Young. After thinking I was the only one using 3x5 cards to organize my daily tasks, someone said, "Oh, you must have read *Side-Tracked Home Executive*." It was their book (it's written by two sisters) that gave me the idea to color code my cards, and showed me how to work monthly chores into my system. It is very funny and well worth reading.

About the Author

Erin Thiele has been blessed to be the mother of four boys, Dallas, Axel, Easton, and Cooper, and three girls, Tyler, Tara, and Macy. Her journey to become the Wise Woman for her daughter began when Tyler was just two-years-old. In 1989, Erin's husband left and eventually divorced her. RMI was founded when Erin searched every denomination in her area but was unable to find the help or hope that she needed.

This book and the workbook *A Wise Woman* were originally one large book she wrote as the Lord led her to prepare her home for her husband's return. Later, this restoration portion of her book was taken out of *A Wise Woman* to help the many women the Lord sent to Erin who were in crisis.

Erin has written many other books with her distinctive style of using the Scriptures to minister to the brokenhearted and the spiritual captives. "He sent **His Word** and healed them, and delivered them from their destructions" (Ps. 107:20).

We have many resources for women to help you no matter what crisis you're in. To find all of her books, please visit: **EncouragingBookstore.com**, or in printed form through **Amazon.com**.

If God is moving in your life and marriage, come to our website and become a member: **RestoreMinistries.net** or **RMIEW.com**.

Also Available

Our Abundant Life Series
on EncouragingBookstore.com & Amazon.com

 Finding the Abundant Life

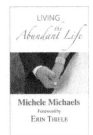 Living the Abundant Life

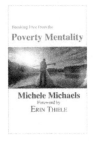 Breaking Free from the Poverty Mentality

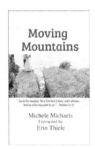
Moving Mountains

Home Schooling for Him: Enter by the Narrow Gate

Please visit our Websites where you'll also find these books as FREE Courses for women.

Our Restore Series
on EncouragingBookstore.com & Amazon.com

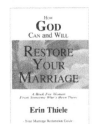

How God Can and Will Restore Your
Marriage: From Someone Who's Been There

A Wise Woman: A Wise Woman Builds Her
House By a FOOL Who First Built on Sinking
Sand

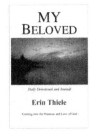

My Beloved: Daily Devotional and Journal
Coming into the Presence and Love of God

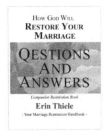

How God Will Restore Your Marriage:
Questions and Answers

 What to Do When Facing Divorce

 Facing Divorce, Again: Enthusiastically and without Fear

Please visit our Websites where you'll also find these books as FREE Courses for women.

By the Word of Their Testimony Series

on EncouragingBookstore.com & Amazon.com

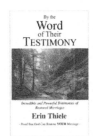
By the Word of Their Testimony: Incredible and Powerful Testimonies of Restored Marriages

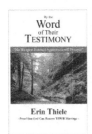
By the Word of Their Testimony: "No Weapon Formed Against you will Prosper"

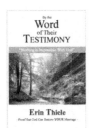
By the Word of Their Testimony: "Nothing is Impossible with God"

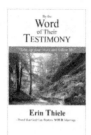

By the Word of Their Testimony: "Take up your cross and follow Me"

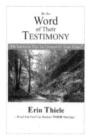

By the Word of Their Testimony: "He Will Give you the Desires of Your Heart"

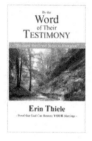

By the Word of Their Testimony: "Proclaim the Good News to Everyone"

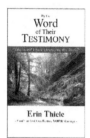

By the Word of Their Testimony: "Proclaim the Good News to Everyone"

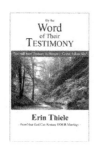

By the Word of Their Testimony: "You will have Treasure in Heaven–Come, follow Me"

Books for Men

on EncouragingBookstore.com & Amazon.com

How God Will Restore Your Marriage:
There's Healing After Broken Vows: A Book
for Men

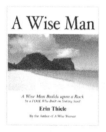

A Wise Man: A Wise Man Builds upon a Rock
by a Fool Who Built on Sinking Sand

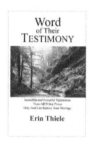

Word of Their Testimony: Incredible and
Powerful Testimonies From MEN that Prove
Only God Can Restore Your Marriage

Please visit our Websites where you'll also find
these books as FREE Courses for both men and
women:

Restore Ministries International

POB 830 Ozark, MO 65721 USA

For more help
Please visit one of our Websites:

EncouragingWomen.org

HopeAtLast.com

LoveAtLast.org

RestoreMinistries.net

RMIEW.com

RMIOU.com

Aidemaritale.com (French)

AjudaMatrimonial.com (Portuguese)

AyudaMatrimonial.com (Spanish)

Pag-asa.org (Tagalog Filipino)

UiteindelikHoop.com (Afrikaans)

ZachranaManzelstva.com (Slovak)

EncouragingMen.org

Made in United States
Orlando, FL
24 May 2022

18152053R00114